D1395092

DARK
DESTROYER

DARK
DESTROYER

NIGEL BENN

BLAKE

Published by Blake Publishing Ltd,
3 Bramber Court, 2 Bramber Road, London W14 9PB, England

First published in hardback in Great Britain 1999

ISBN 1 85782 3087

British Library Cataloguing-in-Production Data:
A catalogue record for this book is available
from the British Library.

Typeset by BCP

Printed and bound by in Great Britain by
Creative Print and Design (Wales), Ebbw Vale, Gwent

3 5 7 9 10 8 6 4

Every effort has been made to contact the
copyright-holders, but some were untraceable.
We would be grateful if the relevant owners could contact us.

Pictures reproduced by kind permission of
Alpha, Colorsport, Allsport, Allsport/Vandystadt.

CONTENTS

AUTHOR'S NOTE

The first draft of this book was written five years ago. As you will understand when you read it, my life was very complicated then, and I decided at the time that I did not want to publish it.

That first version could not have been written without the help and skill of John Lisners, and this final version has been based on his original work. I would like to thank him for his contribution.

Nigel Benn, 1999

I dedicate this book to my wife,
who has stood by me through everything.
I will always be in debt to you.
There is nobody I love more than you.
Thank you for being there for me.

PROLOGUE
25 FEBRUARY 1995

'You have to go to war, and in war you have to be prepared to die. That's what boxing is.'

Gerald McClellan,
Thursday, 23 February 1995

'Let's go to work ...' My corner man gave me the word and I nodded. We left my room. I was dressed in black shorts and black boots, a Clint Eastwood-type poncho covering my body. My blood was boiling, and I was psyched up like never before — ready to go out there and do some damage to the man they all said was going to hammer me.

Do you know how much noise 12,000 people can make? The roar of the crowd brought goosebumps to my flesh. It was so loud you might have thought the roof of the stadium was going to burst. Man, I was buzzing, and when I raised my hands in the air, the crowd went wild — I knew then that they were on my side. We were like gladiators, ready to fight until one of us dropped.

Gerald McClellan, the challenger, was already in the ring. He was the most ferocious fighter ever to hit our shores, a freak of nature. I heard later he'd been shooting his mouth off, bragging about how he was going to finish me off quickly. But I don't read those pre-match reports; you never know how they're going to affect you. In my mind he was just an obstacle in my way — there was £700,000 at stake and he had to be removed.

The bell went for the start of the first round. When I got into the ring, I thought to myself, 'Yeah the arms don't look so bad, legs are skinny.' I didn't even think about being scared of the man until I felt his punch. Man, I didn't know where I was; I didn't know a guy could hit that hard. I went straight through the ropes. I clambered back into the ring, but he kept at me, bashing me from pillar to post. By the end of the first round, I was a mess.

When the bell finally sounded, my corner man Dennie Mancini took over the show. He grabbed me and said, 'Fucking hell, Nigel, you've really got him in trouble, mate!'

But I'm bashed to pieces! What's he talking about, I've got him in trouble? When I heard what Dennie said, though, it turned it all around for me.

'Really? Yeah, too right, Den, he is in trouble.' That was just what I needed to pick me up. If I'd had some guy in the corner saying, 'Look, Nige, you're taking a battering here,' then my morale's going to plummet. But thanks to Dennie, I went into the second round feeling like a champion, and now it's me bashing him around, me making him run. *Bang!* Come on, mate, I don't care what you throw at me.

In the second, I had him running round the ring with half his gum-shield hanging out. Everyone was going crazy. I was throwing big hooks and he was on his back foot.

At the end of round eight he put me down. I hardly knew what hit me, but I just thought, 'Yeah, that's good. Now feel one of mine!' I got up, he rushed in towards me, and I gave him a right uppercut and a left hook. I'd regained the initiative, and I could feel that the fight was mine. I put him down twice, and then a final right uppercut brought him to his knees. I remember saying, 'When you come up for round fucking nine, there's going to be more of that!' The crowd went wild, and I screamed, 'WHO IS HE? WHO'S THE CHAMPION?'

The ref stopped the fight in the tenth round; McClellan was just sitting in the corner. I didn't know what was wrong with him. My head was spinning, and I was so bashed up I wasn't even sure if I had won. It wasn't until I felt my arm being lifted into the air that I knew I'd done it.

The next thing I knew, my dad was there. He gave me a pat on the back that nearly knocked me to the floor. Then there was a television camera.

'They brought him over here to try to bash me up,' I shouted at the interviewer. 'Look at him now!'

The roar of the crowd was still deafening.

And then I blacked out with the pain. The whole thing hadn't lasted longer than 20 minutes. I woke up in an ambulance with my wife Carolyne beside me, crying her eyes out. Man, the pain was wracking my body, but I managed to turn to her and smile.

'You want to go out partying?' I whispered. Somehow she managed to smile despite her tears.

I ended up in the London Hospital in the same ward as McClellan. The man had done me some serious harm — I had a fractured nose and jaw, and I was passing blood because of the kidney damage. But McClellan wasn't even awake. I managed to hobble over to his bed where I looked at him, kissed him, and said simply, 'Sorry.'

That was my ultimate fight, and let me tell you something —inflicting that kind of damage does something to you. Sure, I'd wanted to win, but not at this price. I'd helped nurse Michael Watson after Chris Eubank did the same to him back in 1991, and the nightmare for me now was that Gerald wouldn't recover. On that night in 1996, my heart went out of boxing, the sport that had been my life for the previous ten years. Even Sadé, my little girl, could see the wreck that her daddy had become, and whispered softly for me to retire.

And so I did. Sure, there were a few more fights, but I'd given it everything I had. That fight was the last chapter in the story of the Dark Destroyer, and the first in the story of my new life. Now it's time to tell everyone how it is, to tell the truth about the fights, the women, the money.

I'm Nigel Benn, the Dark Destroyer, two-time champion of the world. This is my story ...

1

ANDY WON'T BE COMING HOME AGAIN

I was eight when I heard the devastating news. Even at that tender age, I knew my world would never be the same again. Andy was lying on a table in the mortuary and my dad had to identify his body. He was just 17. Drained of life. A warrior at peace with the world.

Andy was my god. He was my eldest brother and the bond linking us had grown far beyond the usual blood ties that exist between siblings and had progressed into a form of sincere love and adulation. He had been a hero to whom I could reach out and touch. He was handsome, powerful and invincible. A conqueror. A charismatic knight. Never mind that he threw me out of the top bunk in our cramped bedroom when tiring of my games, or that he cut a race track into my head. Andy could do no wrong. I would feel safe and contented snuggling up to his strong frame, gently bringing my lips to his face and daring to lick or suck his eyebrow while stroking his cheek.

The outside world, the suburban jungle of Ilford with its row upon row of terraced houses, corner shops, cafés, police stations and street gangs, had formed a different opinion. Andy spelled trouble — *big* trouble. He was too tough for his own good, and it was out of respect for his strength that small armies would have to take him on in a street fight. One brave youth against many. The police, too, had grudgingly bowed to his physical superiority by once sending seven officers to arrest him at home. On that occasion he demanded, and was granted, the dignity of being allowed to walk unhindered to the Black Maria, free of handcuffs and without being escorted, pushed and shoved by over-zealous or bullying policemen.

There were many who had predicted that he would come to no good. My mum, Mina, and dad, Dickson, were to regret the fact that they had not insisted Andy remain permanently in Shorey Village, St Andrew, Barbados when Dad emigrated to England in 1956. A year later, Mum followed Dad, leaving Andy behind to be brought up by our grandmother while my parents established themselves in London. This was quite a common occurrence among West Indian people who could rely on an extended family for support.

Dad was 23 when he arrived here, and Mum was 19, both of them hoping to find a land of opportunity. Most of his best mates had already sailed or were about to sail to Britain. Like him, they were hard-working, honest folk who wanted the best for their families and were prepared to slog it out doing menial jobs in order to better themselves and provide careers for the children.

When the boat train rumbled into Victoria, Dad was dismayed with his first impression of London. He thought he'd made a disastrous mistake and wished there was another train to take him straight back home. It was March and he couldn't understand why he'd been so daft as to leave the Caribbean for a dirty, mucky, cold country.

In fact, it was only a short time after Dad's arrival in London that Andy was born in Barbados, so he never saw his first-born son until he was eight years old. Those were difficult times. After the war years and before independence, people didn't starve in Barbados. They might have gone hungry but they would not starve and they didn't have to rely on shops for their provisions. They grew a lot of their own food and flying fish, a staple diet, was cheap and plentiful. As British passport holders, Barbadians had every right to settle in Britain and came here to earn more money and create better lives for themselves than was possible in the West Indies.

Back in Shorey Village, in the northern part of Barbados, Dad had worked on sugar cane plantations during harvest time and had also trained as a carpenter. However, the thought of being a chippy in Britain and having to endure the freezing cold didn't appeal to him very much so he chose an engineering job with British Rail.

In those days, it was easy to change jobs and Dad eventually ended up in Ilford, Essex, working for such companies as J Burns, which supplied car parts for the big automobile manufacturers. One of their sidelines was to make ceiling tiles. He became an expert at this and was promoted to foreman. He stayed with them for 15 years until he was made redundant, and then joined Ford Motors in Dagenham, building engines. He was a supervisor for 14 years until his retirement at the end of 1992. He has always said that if he had had his time over again, he would have joined the Metropolitan Police.

Like Dad, Mum never stopped working. Even now she works evenings as a cleaner at the hospital where I was born. I've told her many times that she needn't bother as I would help her out financially but she's not interested. Both of my parents have a very strong work ethic thanks to the tough times they knew when they first arrived.

They bought their house in Henley Road, Ilford, in 1960 and still live there. I guess it holds too many memories for them to move, even though I've tried to coax them away. In those early days, there were times when Dad was so skint that he would come home in despair, not knowing where he was going to get his next penny. Yet somehow they managed. He would also take on second jobs at night to make ends meet.

I give them full credit for their efforts. They deserve a medal. They never took anything from the state and paid for their own house and fed and clothed seven boys. Dad, who is a born-again Christian, but was not overly religious when we were little, would pray to God for strength and good health.

'Please, Lord,' he'd say, 'please let me live long enough to see my boys grow up. After that, even if I die the next day, I will be happy and grateful that you let me live this long.'

Andy was about 11 when they finally sent for him. He was running wild and our grandparents had begged Mum and Dad to relieve them of the responsibility of looking after him.

When he arrived, we totalled seven brothers living in a three-bedroom terraced house in Henley Road, Ilford, Essex. It was about 12 miles from the West End of London and both Mum and Dad had saved, slaved and sweated to buy it, sometimes taking on two jobs at once in order to give us a home we could call our own.

Andy had traded palm trees, sugar cane fields and the tropical sea for a patch of grey suburbia in east London. It must have torn his world apart to arrive as a stranger in a foreign land into a family and home to which he intimately belonged but where he also felt totally alien. Even so, the pecking order of the brothers was quickly redefined and Andy became firmly entrenched as our number one.

But he wanted more than just to stay at home arguing with his brothers. That was never going to satisfy his passion for excitement and physical release. Both of these demands were partially catered for by his friends who roamed the streets of Ilford, and Andy quickly became a force to be reckoned with. By the time my brother was 17, he had been in and out of Borstal, caused palpitations for Mum and Dad and had got himself a girlfriend who was more than twice his age.

When I remember Andy, I think to myself, 'He who lives by the sword, dies by the sword.' But I never really found out what happened to him the day he died. To this day, we have not been told the full story. The sketchy details I have been able to piece together still bother me and if ever I should discover that some individual is responsible for what happened to Andy, then God help that person — they'll have Nigel Benn to answer to.

We were told that Andy had been visiting his girlfriend and that there had been a disturbance at her house. There is a suggestion that a number of people had grouped together in another room and that Andy considered a quick escape to be preferable to an unfairly matched battle. He is said to have leapt from an upstairs window, hoping to clear a glass conservatory roof and land in the garden from where he could jump over the back fence. In his rush, he fell through the conservatory roof, shattering the glass and severing a main artery in his groin. Did anyone try to help him as he bled to death? That is another question that continues to trouble me but may never be answered. We all wept for him then and I still grieve for him now.

There have been times when I have thought very seriously of joining him prematurely, to hold him close to me once more. If death means that there is a chance of being with my brother again, then I am tempted towards that unknown journey. Sometimes, when things have been harder than they are now, I felt like ending my life in the hope that I would find consolation with Andy. I wanted to be with him and cuddle him as I had done before he left me. I still dream about him and I guess until I meet him again, my life will be an unfinished chapter. I don't care when death comes or what fate has in store, as long as I can see my brother.

Mum and Dad told us to remember Andy as he was and for that reason not one of us six surviving brothers went to the funeral. In fact, to this day our parents have not revealed the whereabouts of his grave in Barkingside Cemetery, although they visit the spot themselves.

My memory of him is as strong and poignant today as it was when I was eight years old. It is of a well-built, handsome youth who always wore crew-neck jumpers, brown corduroy trousers and Doc Martin boots. He was no big-time criminal. Sure, he was someone who knew how to look after himself but, most importantly, he meant everything to me. He may have got into some bad company but, generally, he was only guilty of minor misdemeanours. As for me? I wanted to be like my idol — a street fighter. The toughest of them all. Just like Andy.

I weighed in at 6lb 4oz at precisely 9.30am on Wednesday, 22 January 1964. It was an unusually mild winter's day, but the good weather was little consolation for the misery my parents suffered. My entry into the world was a total anti-climax. I was born the wrong sex!

What a way to begin life. I was a disappointment to my parents before I'd barely had a chance to draw my first breath. Mum had pinned her hopes on me wearing frilly pink knickers. She and Dad had been praying for a little girl and this time — having already had five boys — they were convinced that their prayers would be answered.

That just shows what a lottery life can be. Had my parents given birth to a girl after their first two sons, they might well have called it a day and not had any more children. I guess there are probably a lot more people out there who also wish I'd been born a girl.

My dad later told us why he and Mum were so convinced I would be female. Quite simply, they were conned by a gypsy woman who came knocking on the door of our Ilford home two months before I was due. She'd probably heard about us from a mutual acquaintance, because she told Dad, 'You have five sons and your wife is expecting another child. This time your baby will be a little girl.'

Dad jumped with joy. He was ecstatic, delirious and grateful. To reward this herald of good news, he went rummaging about the house for money and flowers and gave the gypsy woman his last few pence. In 1964, that amount of money was very important to him and could mean the difference between eating a proper meal or not eating at all. But that didn't matter in the least. This was what my parents wanted to hear and believe.

When, some time later, my mum gave birth to me, Dad rang her at King George's Hospital from a public phone booth. Guessing the worst from the tone in her voice, he said, 'Go on, tell me it's another boy.'

Mum responded in the repentant tones of a sinner at confessional. 'Yes, it's a boy,' she whispered.

Dad went berserk. Angrily, he kicked and punched the red telephone kiosk in unbridled fury, hoping it would fall over in the misguided belief that it might help to relieve his frustration. A woman neighbour, who happened to be passing by at that moment, brightly remarked, 'It's another boy, then, Mr Benn?' He gave her a grim look and stormed into the house, muttering that he would be going out in search of the gypsy woman.

Later that day, he visited Mum in hospital and she asked if he was still disappointed with her. He replied, 'I'm disappointed, but not with you.' Apparently, she just smiled and said she was going to be happy with her boys.

When they'd got over the shock of another son, they christened me Nigel Gregory Benn. However, in spite of everything that had happened, they were determined to learn their lesson the hard way and five years later tried once more for a little girl. This time, there was no gypsy woman on whom they could heap disappointment and anger when their seventh son was born.

What a shame we weren't Irish because I learned during my army days in Northern Ireland that the seventh son of a seventh son has special powers.

With hindsight, the number of men in the Benn family should have been expected because Mum's brother had six sons and her sister, five, before she gave birth to a daughter.

Andy was the only child in our family to have been born in Barbados. He was eight years older than me. The rest of us were all born in London. Dermot is five years older than me, then John who is three years older; next is Danny, two years older; Mark, one year; and Anthony, the baby of the family, is almost six years younger than me.

Although they already had five sons when I was born, Mum was still only 26 and Dad 30. It's just as well because they needed to be young, healthy and strong, as it would have been impossible otherwise to feed and control seven boisterous lads, each of whom had the appetite of a horse.

Although we never went hungry, there were lean times and seven lively boys sharing a small three-bedroom house put a strain on everyone. The brothers were forever fighting over food or clothes or just brawling with one another for amusement.

Thankfully, Mum was a genius at making ends meet and creating meals out of virtually nothing, while Dad provided a heavy-handed discipline in an attempt to keep us all on the right side of the law. I always feared his temper if I did wrong. He is a big man, 6ft 1in and powerfully built. Before he whacked us — and he did so only when we deserved it — he would say in a broad West Indian accent, 'If you don't hear it, you must FEEL it.' And feel it I did, far too often for my liking because, when he hit, it was like being struck with the force of an express train.

While today it seems that most parents would be arrested for the type of discipline he administered, I'm grateful for it. Were it not for my father, I'd probably be in prison instead of enjoying success as a world champion.

I sometimes wonder what I would be doing now if my parents had stayed in Barbados. They left behind them enough relatives to fill Wembley Stadium.

Mum tells me I was a good baby. That probably means I didn't cry much, only occasionally sucked my finger and was generally easy to manage. Unfortunately, she was in for a tough time, for my infant years were to be the lull before the storm.

School was never much fun for me. I first went to Woodlands Infant School in Ilford and then to Cleveland Primary, where I was extremely boisterous and grew up well before my time. After that I went — sometimes — to Loxford School, where I took my CSE exams. As a child, I never felt I was a black kid in a white community. There had never been any racism in our family, although we were aware of its existence. Here again, I have to thank the sensible attitude of my parents. They upheld good old-fashioned virtues, which included respect for others, no matter what their creed or colour might be and, at the same time, gave us a feeling of equal standing in the community, so there was never a feeling of inferiority or superiority.

Until the age of eight, the worst thing that happened to me was getting lost at a fairground. I'd wandered off and each of my parents thought I was with the other until they met up and realised I'd disappeared. They were terrified that I might have been abducted and quite overwhelmed when they found me sitting casually on a chair, with my feet up on the table, in the Lost Property office. My mother wept with relief. As for me, I just hadn't a clue what they had been going through and sat there without a care in the world. My other memory of the early years is of being on a school coach, stuffing my face with orange cheese and then being sick on the bus. That experience turned me off orange cheese for good.

While each of us boys had very different personalities, Dad tells me that I was probably a little more steamy than the other kids. I always had to be moving, he would say, and my parents also noticed I had unusually strong vitality and bags of energy. As I grew older, this vitality had to have an outlet and that is when I began treading the same path as Andy.

Looking after myself came naturally with five older brothers. We were always fighting and squabbling, whether it was for food, clothes or out of sheer malice. I guess my first lessons in fighting started at home. We also progressed to such things as lock picking, because Mum would desperately try to eke out the weekly provisions by locking some of them away. Inevitably, we would pick the locks and gorge on the spoils. There would be fights over cans of beans, loaves of bread and milk.

When the food ran out, we'd knock up 'bakes' from flour, water and sugar and sometimes we'd have to live on that for days. Mum would do the week's shopping on a Friday and, if she left it around, it would be gone by Sunday evening. Toast, butter and sugar became another favourite, as did chips and bread.

Although money was hard to come by and there wasn't an abundant supply of food, we brothers somehow managed to dress with style, although this would also lead to fights. Clothes were probably more important to us than food, and from an early age I would admire the way my older brothers dressed and looked. My brother Mark would buy exotic crocodile, lizard and emu skin shoes. They cost a king's ransom but were essential accessories to complement his smart trousers and jackets. These small treasures would all be locked away until another brother decided to pick the locks and borrow the items. On discovery, the inevitable fight would break out, but what else could you expect with up to five brothers sharing one bedroom?

If the fighting became too violent, Andy would protect me from the others. He was by far the toughest of the Benn brood and nobody would take him on lightly. I felt happy and contented in his company and revelled in tales of his street fighting and his daring. I was too young to be judgemental about his actions and too much in awe of him to question his motives. After his death, I cried and cried for him. I missed his warmth and his charisma. I was unwilling to banish him from my mind. I wanted to *be* Andy.

It is possible, if I search my mind and try to be honest, to come to the conclusion that, for the rest of my life, I would seek his replacement. That, at least, is one interpretation that could explain my actions because, after Andy's departure, I befriended much older boys than myself and was determined to be the toughest kid in the neighbourhood. From the age of 11 or 12, I would be found in the company of older boys and young men, some of whom were twice my age.

Later, in my professional life, whenever I saw what appeared to be exceptional or Svengali qualities in people, I tended to be impressed by them and, on occasions, fell under their spell until disillusionment set in. At the end of the day, I should have realised that the best people for advice were back in Henley Road — my mum and dad. They are the only ones I really listen to now.

After some expensive and harrowing experiences, I now manage my own affairs and tend to keep people at a distance unless I know them really well. I have been very badly let down and hurt in the past by people to whom I extended my loyalty and friendship within a business relationship. Learning through my errors, and some of them have been very costly, I have become more cynical in my choice of friends and business partners.

Outside my immediate family circle, my first fight was with bare knuckles at a local swimming pool with a kid called Leo Isaacs. I was about nine and Leo was three years older and full of himself. Now he's a good mate of my brother's, but then I just wanted to hit him. He was short, powerful and stocky. I wouldn't like to fight him now because he is really strong and a specialist at holding you in a deadly headlock. But I didn't know that at nine, and I punched him straight in the eye and scored my first victory.

The fights with my brothers were too frequent and too numerous to list, although there were a few memorable ones.

On one occasion, my brother Danny thought he had killed me. We'd been fighting over a can of baked beans when Danny had had enough of me punching him. He grabbed me, held my arms and bit my tongue so hard that his teeth went right through it. (All the scars on my face and head are not from the ring but from injuries sustained when fighting my brothers and members of the public in the streets around Ilford long before I became a boxer.)

When Danny bit me, I was in a state of shock and couldn't talk. However, the wounds healed relatively quickly and soon we were at loggerheads again. This time it started after I'd given him a lot of verbal. I was taking the mickey and he told me to shut up. Kids can be pretty cruel and we were no exception. Danny had once had a fit while eating a toffee. The sight of it was hilarious and will stick in my mind for ever. We'd all watched him sitting in front of a heater, a toffee stuck in his mouth, and his head jerking towards the ceiling and these two large eyes were rolling around uncontrollably. A doctor had been present and was tugging at his ear lobe to bring him to his senses.

After that, we called him Toffee. Adding insult to injury, we would play a version of the TV series *Give Us A Clue* where you mime a scene in a comic fashion and someone has to guess who or what you are enacting. Danny wasn't amused at me parodying his fit while playing this game and when, amid gales of laughter, I refused to stop my antics, he went for me with unexpected aggression.

Seizing me by the neck, he began to choke me. There was no way I could get out of his grip so I relaxed my body and went totally limp in his hands. As he released me, I slumped back in the chair and pretended to be dead. He must have believed he'd killed me because he went screaming into the street, yelling in despair, 'I'VE KILLED NIGEL. I'VE KILLED NIGEL.' Then he came back to find me still in the chair but with both arms raised and two sets of fingers defiantly and offensively extended in a Churchill gesture to maximise the insult. He wasn't sure whether to whack me, throttle me again or kiss me because I was alive.

Most of the family agreed that the similarities between me and Andy were quite uncanny. Mentally, we were almost like identical twins. Perhaps this would explain my restlessness and search for thrills, which followed the same pattern established earlier by my older brother. Why, otherwise, would someone who is surrounded with family love and affection go so determinedly off the rails as I did from about the age of 11? Was I, like Andy, in desperate need of constant physical stimulus through having too much energy, or was I blindly following a role model? Perhaps it was a bit of both.

One thing everyone agreed on, though, was that I was a natural fighter. People with recognised gifts, particularly academics, often find a patron who will ensure that they are given the mental stimulus their brain demands. That usually involves leaving behind playmates with whom they grew up and joining a group much older than themselves. I had no such sponsors and my fighting capabilities were, as yet, unrecognised but, nevertheless, something inside me told me I should find a group of companions much older, tougher and more experienced than myself. I needed that challenge. I also needed to find someone I could respect and model myself on. Another Andy. The time had come for me to grow up.

2

THAT LOVING FEELING

'Oh no, it's the police. Dickson, go and fetch Nigel, he's in trouble again!'

Mum's emotional response to the news that I'd been nicked or was in some kind of trouble was always the same. If I hadn't been waiting in the lock-up I could have whistled her song. The plea for Dad to bail me out had become like the signature tune of a TV soap. With the amount of practice she'd had, Mum was pretty good at reciting it. Nevertheless, it was always sung with mixed feelings: commiseration for the inevitable slap I would get from Dad and frustration at my inability to reform. Contained in those feelings was a pinch of vindictive satisfaction of the 'I told you so' variety and 'Why can't you be like your brother John?'

My brother John was her favourite, Mr Goody Two Shoes, who couldn't put a foot wrong. The contrast between saint and sinner was never greater and there was no question about who was the black sheep of the family. But John's angelic state didn't lessen my love for him. He was always loyal and he was always there and when, later, he encouraged me to become a soldier and join his regiment, he put me on the road to success.

I never felt underprivileged, poor or resentful of those

who had money. If I wanted something badly enough, I'd nick it. It was as simple as that and I never had any great moral dilemma about what I had done. The only fear I had was of Dad finding out. He was the insurmountable obstacle in my path to what might have been a criminal career. Dad could put up with me fighting in the street but he would never condone stealing. That was totally unacceptable to him. If I was caught, the punishment he would hand out was something to be feared. In common with other boys with strict fathers, I used to think that he hated me.

To a slightly-built lad barely into his teens, my father was a giant. His hands were rock solid, with skin like sandpaper, so rough you could light a match on them. If you were on the receiving end of his anger, you'd see more than stars. The night sky would explode and the entire Milky Way would appear, followed by the sun and the moon and, before you knew it, you would be on the floor crying your heart out with pain and self-pity. In my case, I deserved it but, having got that ordeal over, bravado would once more overtake me and, instead of showing remorse, I'd simply vow not to get found out again. Then I would return to the street, displaying my scars like medals from a victorious battle and refuse to show any sign of my earlier penance.

The good thing about my father was that he never weighed himself down with grudges or brooded over the past. Mostly, he thought I was a good lad with loads of energy and spirit, and he didn't want to tame it, he simply wanted to point it in the right direction. We are now the best of friends. I love him and Mum and my children more than anything in the world. If someone ever hurt my family, there would be no question of letting them off the hook. I'd get even no matter how long it might take.

My family means everything to me.

As much as he was able to, Dad supported me at every fight and often accompanied me on training sessions abroad. There is nothing from the past that has destroyed our friendship and love. If anything, the past has cemented the very deep bond which has always existed between us.

When it came to being punished for my wrongs, Dad was absolutely fair. On rare occasions, however, even he would have misgivings about the pain he inflicted, although he would never admit that to me when I was young. There were also times when he tried to reason with me. Like the day he bailed me out on his birthday when I was still in my teens.

Mum had greeted him at the door and he could see black clouds on her face. There was no way she was going to say 'Happy birthday, Dickson.'

He had finished work earlier than normal and had raced home to celebrate. To his dismay, instead of being hugged by Mum, she told him, 'Nigel is in a bit of bother ... Forget the party!' He went mad and said he was going to kill me — murder me. His special day had been ruined and it was all down to me. I'd been short of a few bob and was caught stealing a jacket in a London street market. My timing couldn't have been worse.

The local police asked Dad to collect me and, as soon as he arrived, the arresting officer, who was a bit of a PC Plod, could sense his anger. 'You're in a bad mood,' he said, like some sort of modern-day Sherlock Holmes.

Dad responded a little too positively for my liking. 'Yeah! And I'm about to kill my son.'

Earlier, I had pleaded with the police not to tell my parents. It's quite funny, looking back at it now. I must have seemed like the cartoon character Brer Rabbit, about to be roasted by the fox and pleading for this to happen, rather than be tossed back into the brambles, which was what he really wanted. Unlike the rabbit, however, I really didn't want to be thrown back in the brambles. That meant going home. For all I cared, they could roast me alive so long as they didn't call Dad. I entreated them to let me go or to incarcerate me for ever.

'Just don't phone home,' I begged.

In those days, police never seemed to listen to me and, when Dad showed up, I cheekily asked if I could go home on the bus. Could he lend me eight pence for the fare? I suggested timidly. There was no way I wanted to drive back with him. Thankfully, someone up there had my interests at heart because, after talking to the police officer, he calmed down a bit and we went back together. Instead of giving me the hammering I had expected, he sat down and talked about the way he felt and impressed on me how much he wanted us children to be honest and caring members of society.

I now welcome the discipline he imposed. Although he was pretty strict and we had some tough times together, I respect the fact that he only did it to keep me out of trouble. He always said, 'As a child, I used to get it from my parents, too, and it didn't make me love them any less.' That's my attitude as well and I'm sure it is down to him that I haven't served a prison sentence.

As a child, my father only lost his cool with me once and, boy, did I get it! I'd planned to go to a local fair with some of my mates but needed some readies. The only money available to me at home was the 50p pieces Dad would absent-mindedly leave in his trouser or coat pockets, through which I would furtively search in the hope of scoring some loot. This time his pockets were empty but, next door, at a neighbour's we called Auntie Shirley, a bulging purse was summoning me over. Stealthily, I sneaked into her adjoining house and, after a quick recce, saw the purse stuffed full of pound notes on the table. 'Help me, help me,' it cried out. I could never turn down invitations of this nature and wasted no time in relieving the purse of its contents. I then threw the empty bag into another neighbour's garden and trotted off to the fair, happy as a sandboy. To me, the £15 I had stolen represented a small fortune but it wasn't long before I was discovered on the fair rides, flush with tickets and loaded with sweets and ice-cream. Questioned about my newly-acquired wealth, I lied that I had earned loads of money washing cars.

Judgement day came only a few hours after the theft and it was as theatrical as it was swift. I was scared. So scared that, had it been anybody other than my father judging me, I would have won an Oscar for a top-class performance. A jury would certainly have believed me. Not Dad. I was so fearful of being clobbered that I threw myself on the ground in front of him. To emphasise this humble act of supplication, I then raised myself to my hands and knees with my head and eyes upturned. From my grovelling position I begged him, using a broad Barbadian accent, to bring a stack of Holy Bibles on which I would swear my innocence.

I may as well have implored a block of concrete. The punishment that followed was swift and brutal, far worse than the hurt I would suffer in the ring. I should never have insulted Dad's intelligence because it probably made it worse for me. He got hold of a huge wooden stick wrapped in plastic. It was a million times harder than a truncheon and he smashed it against my leg. He hit me so many times on my left that I cried out for him to hit me on the right. I screamed at him to stop. I couldn't believe the pain. Afterwards he felt bad, almost as bad as I was bruised. He told Mum, 'I nearly broke his leg. I think I went a bit too hard but if I have to keep our son out of trouble, then I will do everything I possibly can.'

My ordeal was not yet over. With his customary

honesty, Dad got out his own money and I was made to go next door, confess my crime and pay back all of Auntie Shirley's money. Beaten and bowed, I limped away with Dad's words ringing in my ears: 'If you can't hear, then you must FEEL.'

Apart from trying to restrain me from wandering too far from the path of righteousness, Dad can be credited with saving my life a month after my twelfth birthday. It was February 1975 and there was no central heating in my room, which I shared with three of my brothers. All we had to keep us warm was a paraffin heater. I was in the top bunk, John was below me and my other brothers, Danny and Mark, were in the next bunk.

In the early hours of the morning, the heater began smouldering and soon clouds of smoke had blackened the ceiling. We were all sound asleep while this drama was unfolding. It would only have been a short time before the lethal effects of oxygen starvation would have snuffed out our lives. Not one of us boys was aware of how close to disaster we were and, to this day, Dad swears it was the hand of God that saved us.

For some inexplicable reason, Dad woke up and was aware of an unusual calm in the house. He felt something was not quite right and lay in his bed for a while, wondering whether he should check the house. After some minutes, he smelt fumes. He sprang out of bed and raced to our room but couldn't see inside. The smoke had become a heavy fog shrouding everything. Desperately, he felt his way to the bunks and heaved us out of the room. Assured that there was no fire, he then checked that we were breathing properly. Happily, we had not been too badly affected by the smoke but had his rescue attempt been delayed by two minutes, there is little doubt that four of his boys would have perished.

Although it became a standing joke that most of Mum's

time was spent bailing me out of trouble at school or in the courts, I was not into crime in a big way. Occasionally, I would shoplift or steal from a street market, but I was never into mugging or burglary. My main preoccupation was having a good time with my friends, listening to music and meeting girls.

I was 11 when Susan Marsh, an Anglo-Indian girl with smouldering looks, olive skin and a Venus figure, waltzed into my life. She was the best thing since sliced bread. She was also my first love at school and, as far as I was concerned, she was breathtakingly beautiful. She was the most sought-after girl in Ilford. I was proud to have her as my girlfriend. For the next three or four years, we had a close but volatile relationship. How I loved her. Then, as now, I was unable to control my emotions. If our friendship became strained, I would be depressed and unhappy and nothing could shake me from my gloom. She knew she had me eating from her hand because whenever she threatened to dump me, I would weep rivers. I had also become quite obsessive about keeping her to myself, even to the point of going into battle to make sure nobody else competed for her love.

As a teenager, my best weapon was my ability to fight with my fists, but occasionally I would carry a baton down my trouser leg. It was like a truncheon and came in very handy, particularly when one of the lads in our circle (I think it was George Small) became too fresh with Susan. Enraged with jealousy, I cracked him in the face with my fist and then hit him with the baton. That put a stop to his flirtation, although a good-looking mate of his, Steve Parker, also fancied her. That caused further problems which I had to sort out using some muscle.

Susan Marsh was too attractive for her own good. In fact, she was so gorgeous that everyone in Ilford fancied her. I genuinely loved her. I still lusted after other girls but I loved her. Towards the end, though, she didn't want to be with me and, eventually, I lost her to a nice, clean-cut black boy who was my opposite. Women have much more power than men and age has got nothing to do with their ability to do your brain in. That, at least, is my experience.

From the age of 12, my best friend was Colin. We hit it off instantly after meeting at the Caribbean Club in Ilford. I think we saw a bit of ourselves in each other and that reflected image made us fight on the very day we met. Nobody won the fight and, as each of us considered ourselves to be Number One, honour was spared. We became close friends from then on. Blood brothers. Colin went to a different school and, while he was the same size as me, he was two years older. We shared the same birthday and, like twins, became inseparable. Colin lived in Ilford. His house has since been knocked down. We were mates almost up to the time I joined the Army and we did absolutely everything together. If one of us couldn't get home, we even slept in the same bed. I was much closer to him than I was to my own brothers.

Colin was the natural leader of our close-knit inner circle, which was completed with Paul and Kevin. When it came to thieving, Paul was the don of all dons. He was the offspring of a hard family and was always trying to make a few quid. He must have served his apprenticeship well because he never went short. Paul was a natural cat burglar, a real professional. We never called him a burglar, though. He was a 'creeper', because he so successfully crept into houses.

He had more bottle than Express Dairies. I could never have done what he did. It made no difference to Paul if the house he had targeted was occupied. In fact, he would welcome the challenge if people were inside. How he got away with it as often as he did is a remarkable feat. He was totally fearless. He was also a good friend and would do anything for you. If you were short of money, having him around was like having your own cash dispenser. Press the right button and he'd provide funds in no time at all.

I remember one particular night when we all wanted to go to a new club near Ilford town centre. As was usually the case, none of us had any money, so Paul crept into a house to get some cash. He was about to steal a handbag from a table when he spotted a guard dog — a massive Great Dane, with long, slimy, yellow fangs that would bring terror to the bravest heart and a gaping hole in your backside. Anybody else, faced with a savage, salivating monster of this beast's proportions, would have given up there and then and tried another house. Not Paul.

Instead of legging it as I would have done, he told us he was going off to find a cat and to wait for him. With that he disappeared into an adjoining garden and minutes later, magician-like, he reappeared holding a struggling ginger tom. The possibility that he might be clawed to pieces made little impact on Paul. He simply announced that this bit of fur was going to be his decoy and serve as bait for the dog.

Paul took it back to the house and waited for the dog to attack him. That guy was so cool. Before the animal could eat him, Paul tossed the ginger cat into its path. That was too much temptation for the Great Dane. It forgot all about Paul and turned its attention to the cat which raced for the nearest fence. It might have been cruel but it was funny to watch. The poor cat looked as though it had been connected to a live cable. Its hair stood on end. It was frozen with fear. Then its instinct for survival brought it back to life and somehow it escaped the frothy jaws of the Great Dane.

In the meantime, having effectively diverted attention away from himself, Paul crept into the house and snatched the handbag. He was about to give us a victory salute from a side door when the dog twigged what was going on and came bounding back. By this time, Paul's body was so full of adrenalin that he sailed over the fence like an Olympic athlete. The dog was left biting air.

Back on the street, Paul was the hero of the moment. His daredevil display had excited and impressed us. We heaped mountains of praise on him before going off to celebrate with his dangerously acquired spoils.

The fourth member of our group was Kevin. At 12, he was already an accomplished pickpocket. Kevin had a way with ladies' handbags, even if they were still attached to the owner. Nature had blessed him with an innocent face. He had the cherubic expression of a choir boy and the manual dexterity of a surgeon. His fingers had become expert in separating valuable items from a secure holding and transferring the same to his back pocket.

While beaming innocently, he would unclip a victim's handbag and enrich himself by ten pounds or more in the process. We'd watch him work the market in Green Lanes, Ilford, where his cover would be to stand in a queue pretending to buy apples or other goods. Even if he was caught red-handed, his innocent looks would get him off the hook. All he would suffer was a stern warning and, providing he bit his bottom lip and hung his head in shame, they'd let him go.

Beyond our small group, we had a host of mates and acquaintances, some close and others more distant. All were part of a brotherhood who belonged and fought together on the streets of east London. Of our close friends, Paul was the most charismatic. He was also smart, tough and handsome. Together, we made a formidable team, whether at play in girls' bedrooms or doing damage to other gangs. Colin was the one I would look up to. He could make difficult things look easy. He got whatever he wanted and he was intelligent as well as smart. On top of all that, he had style and, at that age, he was probably more successful as a stud than I was.

Because we enjoyed each other's company so much, we would generally meet girls in pairs so that we could be together all the time. Throughout our friendship, we always tried dating together. If our girlfriends were mates like we were, that was a dream ticket. Colin and I seemed to keep out of trouble with the law for most of the time. Occasionally, we'd be chased down the street for shoplifting but that came low on our list of priorities. We were really more into girls and having a good time. We were just kids enjoying life.

I made love when I was 12. She was a year older and had been resisting my clumsy offer of 'going all the way' for some months, but I couldn't wait for the rest of my life. I had reached puberty early. There were my new mates to think of, too. The older guys I had been getting friendly with were young men who were up to ten years older than me and had been going with women for years.

This group pressure, particularly as far as the older boys were concerned, had made me all the more determined that it was time I followed their example and lost my virginity. Conveniently, her friend had fallen for Colin and he had been putting similar pressure on her. The girls had kept us dangling on the line for a long time — around six months. We must have finally worn them down because they finally agreed to full sexual intercourse. I could never figure out, though, why it should have been all right after six months. To my mind, it would have been fine on the first day! But still, better late than never.

The big event took place at Colin's home while his parents were out. Colin and I used to wear the same clothes — flared jeans, T-shirts and 50p trainers that looked good when new but were generally worn out by the next day. For this special occasion, we wore our regulation denims which had been nicely washed and ironed, and we'd soaked ourselves in cheap aftershave which you could smell half a mile away. It didn't matter. I was only 12 and was about to embark on a new adventure, an initiation into a new way of life. A real world where grown-up boys made love to grown-up girls.

We never bothered to find out if the girls thought about it in this way, or if they thought about it at all. You don't normally discuss your thoughts and feelings when you are 12 or 13 years old. And you certainly don't ask those questions of girls who are not entirely certain of what they are doing, but are prepared to go with the flow.

Until that moment, no amount of chat had made them change their mind. I would say to Lee, 'I can't wait any more. My dick isn't going to get any harder than it is and if we go on like this much longer, I'm going to fall down. My nuts are getting heavier by the day and I'm going to have to cart them around in a wheelbarrow.'

Thinking back on it, I can picture her exactly as she looked. She was every man's fantasy. She wore tight-fitting jeans, her prettiness enhanced by bright red lipstick, and her breasts were firm and swollen with excitement. What's more, she should have been in a school uniform and a gym slip rather than dressed like a teenage temptress. She was 13 but had the body of a young woman. Sadly, the finer points of this sexuality were probably lost on me as a 12-year-old. But she was as eager as me was to find out about love, even if it meant losing her virginity.

Style usually only comes with money and the usual way of getting about in those days was either by walking or using public transport. The girls rode to womanhood on the number 25 bus. They came around to the house giggling nervously, excited by the prospective guilt and adventure of the occasion. Colin took his girl's hand and led her upstairs. I stayed downstairs in the living room with mine, waiting for their door to slam shut. As soon as we were alone, I nervously took hold of her and kissed her.

This was it. The big moment. I started undoing the buttons of her jeans. Unable to contain myself, I lost patience with the unbuttoning and yanked off her trousers. I was too excited to care if I tore them or any other item of clothing she wore. Timidly she helped me off with my trousers and then we raced each other to see who would be the first to be fully naked. We lost our virginity in about two seconds flat. Thinking back on it now, I would give myself a sexual rating of nought out of ten.

Over the years, I would like to think that I have improved 100 per cent in my love-making. I no longer just try to please myself, but am far more intent on pleasing my partner. On that first occasion, however, I was a selfish boy. There was no romance. It had been a purely sexual experience. But the explosion I felt when making love was out of this world. It was like 'Hey, the world's just blown up and I enjoyed it.' I wanted more. Much more. And I wanted it regularly.

I didn't ask her if she wanted to do it again after I had regained my composure and the dust had settled from the atomic explosion. After my shamefully fast performance — I admit to having been a premature ejaculator when I lost my virginity — we just did it again as if it was the natural thing to do. The second time left me drained but happy. The experience had been phenomenal and the mental high I'd experienced was something new to me. I was convinced a chemical reaction had taken place in my brain. It had. I was hooked on sex!

3

THE GOOD, THE BAD
AND THE UGLY

Most of the teachers at Loxford School were unanimous about my future; they reckoned I had none. They predicted I would end up collecting handouts in a dole office. Understandably, we held each other in contempt. But there were two exceptions: the maths mistress Miss Dorothy Baker, and the PE teacher John Salisbury. Both of them liked me and recognised that I had some kind of potential to be developed.

I liked school only because it meant being with friends and having some fun. My attendance was acceptable, my attitude questionable. Among my best mates at school were Barry Hayden, Garry Clarke, Leon Jackson, Michael Hedley, Derek Miller and Paul Augustin, whom we called Bethel. Since school, we have gone our separate ways.

Although it would have been simple for me to bunk classes, I preferred going because it was more fun being with my buddies. My physical and mental development virtually decreed that I become the school bully and I was also the most disruptive boy in class. At one point, I was virtually expelled but given a second chance on condition that I attended a support unit for disturbed or difficult kids.

I spent six months there as a cooling-off period. The hours were great. A late start in the mornings, around ten, and you got off by three in the afternoon. The disadvantages were that it was separate from the main school and further to travel to and I was away from my classmates. Another negative factor was the attitude of a few of the teachers. They would treat you as if you were mentally deranged. I couldn't believe it. They talked to me as if I was some kind of nutter. Worse still, I realised there actually were quite a number of genuine head-cases there.

One of the pupils was certifiably mad. He had a vacant, twisted face, the type you would imagine belonged to the village idiot in medieval Britain. He'd do stupid things to amuse himself and get away with it because he was nuts. During one tea break, he sneaked up behind me, lifted a solid oak chair high above his head and nearly brought it crashing down on me. He was an idiot, completely and utterly loopy. If I hadn't stopped him, the blow would have broken my back.

If you became bored in this 'asylum', you could pretend to be nutty yourself and, providing you were docile, they would listen to imaginary problems and ask ridiculous questions until you tired of the game. I was 14 but the way teachers talked down to us, I might as well have been six. 'Now, what did you do at school today?' they would ask sympathetically, wondering if you had difficulty understanding them.

I'd look around and see people staring into space. Some had their mouths open. Had the world gone mad? Sometimes it was hard to distinguish the staff from the pupils. The place spooked me out. It was weird. There were lots of kids from broken homes as well as some who'd been abused. I had one friend there, though, who reminded me of a Steve McQueen character. He seemed pretty normal and we always had a laugh. He also provided relief from the boredom by constantly getting into fights.

After six months in purgatory, I returned to the main

school. Nothing had changed. I was back to my disruptive self within days and a tiresome flow of expulsion threats once more began dropping through our letterbox. It was as if the Benn family were sending a faulty product to school and it prompted a series of complaints: 'Mr. Angry from Loxford School writes again ...' Obviously, they considered me to be one of a bad batch which they were desperate to reject. Anyway, one of my parents would always turn up at the school pleading my case and assuring them that the product was sound. Poor Mum and Dad. I gave them a tough time.

English and maths were my best subjects but I hated history and electronics. I'm proud to be British but I couldn't relate to English history. It meant very little to me. What did Richard the Lionheart or Robin Hood have to do with me? I was sure I was a couple of shades darker than Robin Hood. I wanted to learn a lot more about my own background. History should be meaningful.

My family in the West Indies had been sold into slavery centuries ago. Was there a white trader or plantation owner in our bloodline? I was told a lot of them couldn't keep their dicks inside their trousers. What were my family's origins? What hardships did my ancestors endure as a result of slavery? Was this why we are a strong race today, because only the fittest could survive the harsh conditions imposed by their masters? These were significant historical matters which were not covered in our boring syllabus.

On the sports field, however, I came into my own. I was a natural athlete, the best in school at cross country, pole vaulting, the long jump and running 1500 metres.

My favourite subject was fighting, but that wasn't taught in class. I learnt it in the streets and in clubs where they practised kung fu and other forms of martial arts. Bruce Lee was all the rage. He was my film idol. I was captivated and totally inspired by his fighting skills. I wanted to be Bruce Lee.

While the head teacher considered me disruptive and a danger to other pupils, my father argued that I was only letting off steam. What Dad wanted was for them to offer a constructive outlet for my inexhaustible energy. If I was to blame for my behaviour, then they were equally at fault for not recognising my potential and harnessing it to our mutual benefit.

Dad had always hoped that one of his boys would make something of his life. He had a sneaking suspicion that it might be me because he remembered how I had always insisted that I would one day be famous. Ever since I was a small boy, I had told him I would drive a Rolls-Royce or a Porsche when I grew up. And he was quite sure that if success came, it would be through sport.

Whatever ambitions he might have held for me, school was not the place to air them. Loxford didn't know how to handle Nigel Benn. They didn't seem to agree with Dad's suggestions or his explanations about my boisterous behaviour. As a teenager, I did not appreciate my own strength. Dad, on the other hand, was well aware of it, and he was very worried about the damage I might inflict. After all, he had inside knowledge. He'd seen it all happen at home. My younger brother Anthony, a good-looking little boy, had had his head sliced open like a watermelon after a mock kung fu battle in which we used long pieces of wood. And although I'd dished it out on that occasion, I was always at the local hospital myself having parts of my body stitched together.

Once I was booted, smashed and slammed into a brick wall. Afterwards, my head was dented into a U-shape. It was my fault. I'd been too mouthy to Michael Davidson, whose mother owned the corner shop. He was really like a big brother and used to take us to football matches. He'd let us clear the shop of sweets for five pence but could occasionally play rough.

Once I started going out with the older boys, my confidence grew out of all proportion to my years. By 13, I'd become quite punchy and if someone dared to touch me, I'd knock their head off. If I was walking down Ilford High Street and someone offended me, they would never repeat it. The fact that I wasn't scared of anyone worried my father. He told me to cool down. 'You just don't recognise your strength. It's getting you a bad reputation. People are becoming frightened of you,' he warned. I would fight anybody, no matter how big they were.

After he'd been summoned to school following yet another punch-up, Dad turned to me and said, 'If you've got that much energy, get in the boxing ring and do it for real.' That was quite prophetic because I had been in a ring only once in my life. My brother John had arranged for me to have a try-out when I was 12. They put me in with a guy who'd been boxing since he was five years old and apparently I panned him all round the ring. My opponent ended up with a blotchy-red complexion and the 'fight' had to be stopped. John told me then that I was a natural. 'You're a born fighter,' he said. He took me to the gym a few more times but I showed little interest. I was much more into martial arts at the time.

Despite Dad's advice, I could never imagine that, one day, I would make a career of boxing. I'd have been the last person to believe it. But perhaps the seed had been planted, along with a warning. While he acknowledged my skill as a fighter, Dad cautioned me, 'You'll be a dead man if you try it on me.'

In spite of that, he backed me all the way when another expulsion threat was made. Dad was sick of the letters complaining about me. He'd had enough. He steamed into the head teacher, 'I'd like you to listen to me for a change. You're picking on my son. You're a *racist*. I'm sick of your letters. A lot of kids at your school don't understand that Nigel has so much energy. He's only playing with the kids. He doesn't know his own strength.'

The headmaster was in no way a racist, and wasn't very happy at being called one, but both he and Dad calmed down and shook hands after their heated exchange. My position was not vastly improved by the showdown. The letters stopped coming for a while but, before long, I was up to my old tricks again.

The main difficulty was that I had outgrown the kids at school. Even at home, because of my ability to look after myself, my parents had given me much greater leeway than they did my older brothers. I was allowed to stay out later than them, and more often, and they were less worried about me if I didn't return on time. I also had a lot more street cred than my brothers, through mixing with much older boys.

Loxford School may not have liked me then but they would always remember me. In fact, I warm to the idea that even if I hadn't been a success in the ring, they would still have remembered me. And if that memory may have been a little soured, it wouldn't have bothered me in the least. I'd rather be a somebody than a nobody. I bet all the good boys who kept their heads down and swotted hard for A-levels have long been forgotten.

Old wounds are quickly healed when there is the chance to rub shoulders with fame. Had I been serving ten years for a crime — and there was a strong possibility of this at one stage of my life — my teachers would probably have nodded wisely and said, 'We told you so. We knew that boy would come to no good.' But as a world champion boxer they were proud to have me return as an old boy. When I was invited to address the school after leaving, they lined up to shake my hand. They even asked me to attend one of the teacher's funerals. I still visit Miss Baker who stood by me all those years ago.

After addressing assembly and chatting to various staff members, I wondered if any of them recalled the time when one of the teachers wanted me arrested. That happened a couple of days before my fifteenth birthday, when the local police received an urgent invitation to visit the school. They arrived with sirens blaring after being told that a pupil had obtained money using threats. I had devised what I considered a brilliant plan to acquire instant riches on my birthday.

Financial circumstances being as they were, I could not rely on sackfuls of presents from home so I turned my attention to my school chums. I figured that if everybody in school brought 50p as a birthday gift, it would be like winning a mini lottery. In the past, I had gently persuaded students to bring me small peace offerings. These included a bike, a skateboard and running shoes, all of them freely handed over. Nobody had the guts to say no to the toughest kid in school.

I was determined to make my fifteenth birthday memorable. By that age I'd figured out that people only give you presents if they love you, respect you or want something from you. I worked on the respect angle. Because my birthday was due on Sunday, I told everyone to bring a present before the weekend. Moreover, I let it be known that if respect was not shown in the form of a shiny 50p piece, those withholding might have serious regrets. The fear factor worked a treat. Silver coins rained from heaven. I'd hit the jackpot. A sack so full of money that I could hardly lift the thing. My mate helped to keep an eye on the stash which we hid under my desk. During the lesson, my mind concentrated on how I would spend this bonanza. Unfortunately, my spendthrift fantasies came to an abrupt end. One of the form mistresses called me out of the class.

Somebody had grassed and she accused me of extorting

money with threats. I protested my innocence and tried to convince her that each coin was a gift for a popular classmate. When she called the police, my only regret was that they would seize the money. I'd never had so much. Watching it disappear was heartbreaking. Couldn't they let me keep it a bit longer? Parting with it reminds me of the film *Ghost* in which Whoopi Goldberg briefly gets her hands on $4 million but is told to give it away to New York nuns collecting for charity. Like her, I could have screamed in despair.

I was brought to my senses when they told me they were phoning my dad. Have you ever seen a black man turn white? Well, that's what happened next because, in spite of my protests, they called my father. As far as I was concerned, they might as well have asked me to start digging my grave. Dad managed to iron matters out but, for some reason, didn't whack the living daylights out of me.

The centre of our universe was the Mocca Bar, a café in Ilford. When I was not at school I practically lived there, particularly over weekends. It is now called the Rainbow, which is under different ownership, and is a very different kind of place. It was owned by a real character called Jimmy. He was an Alex Higgins lookalike who would scream abuse at you if you gave him a hard time. In fact, you wouldn't even have to abuse him. He was always screaming and shouting. He had a bad temper but a kind heart.

The Mocca was always a hive of activity. It was like the Old Vic pub in the TV soap *EastEnders*. Deals were made, meetings arranged and goods exchanged. Petty villainy was discussed over an orange juice or a weak cup of tea, after which the conspirators would play pinball machines or tug at an illicit joint in a dark corner.

However, there was little honour among thieves. Despite the beating I'd got over Auntie Shirley's purse, I nicked another one in a jeans shop near Cranbrooke Park some time later. There was twice as much money in this one and I couldn't believe my luck. Like an idiot, I boasted about my rich pickings at the Mocca Bar and, by the end of the evening, someone had pickpocketed me! I cried at the loss of my ill-gotten gains. It just shows that you should never show a thief you've got money.

Those days are well behind me, although I've never forgotten the crowd who used the Mocca. Half of them are jealous, envious that I've made a few bob and say I should go down there and give them some money and buy a few drinks. I'd like to shoot them instead. All they can do is ponce. Why don't they get off their backsides and do something? I don't respect dossers who won't work or who won't try to achieve something in life. No one has it easy. I had to get off my butt to succeed. Some of them have turned into old women.

I had my first experience with drugs at the Mocca Bar. I smoked some cannabis, which I didn't particularly like, and later made the mistake of telling my girlfriend, Susan Marsh, about it. My best mate Colin and Susan were at my house at the time and I'd been a bit boisterous. Playing silly games, I smashed a milk bottle over Colin's knee and glass went flying everywhere. Susan told me that if I didn't stop mucking about she'd tell my dad that I smoked weed. I replied that she wouldn't dare and then took her home, leaving the broken bottle on the floor. She and I had a fight on the way because she wanted to finish our relationship and I was very upset about it. In fact, she was quite physical in her approach. She kicked me in the shins and slapped my face.

I returned home, absolutely gutted, to be confronted by Dad. 'What's this then?' he asked. Thinking he meant the broken glass, I offered to pick it up. 'No,' he said menacingly. 'What's this about draw? You think you're a big man now?' And with that he slapped me with his open hand. I swear it was as solid as being knocked down by a truck. He knocked me into tomorrow and battered me around, left, right and centre. It was time for a quick exit, I thought, and escaped back to Susan's. I thought she'd been a real bitch and spilled the beans. In fact, she hadn't said anything. Dad had overheard me boasting about the draw.

Nearly all of my older friends were as tough as hardened steel. My mentor was Carl Marston. I admired him so much that I allowed him to step into my brother Andy's shoes. He not only looked like Andy but he reminded me of him in so many other ways. He was a survivor and an unbeaten street fighter. He was always wheeling and dealing and ducking and diving. He was a street man's man. Handsome, fearless and cool as an ice cube.

Even stronger than Carl was Owen Johnson, whom we called Bully. I'd never do a round with Bully. He'd murder me. If I did have to fight him, I'd either leg it or shoot him, except that the bullets would probably bounce off him. He's a doorman in the West End and I felt very sorry for anyone who picked a fight with him.

Sledge was another mate. His real name was Howard Brown and I'm not quite sure where he ended up. He used to make me cry by hammering my head with his fist. Sledge probably thought my body was a post and he was power-driving it into the ground. That might sound funny if you're not on the receiving end, but I invariably was.

They were all hard men but we called those three the Good, the Bad and the Ugly. Carl was the good, Bully the bad, and Sledge the ugly.

The wider circle included Six-Finger Scotty (he was born with six fingers), Daniel and Nigel Nelson, Lloyd and Richard Ramsey, Carl Mosely, Mousey and Andy Coward. Most of them came from Manor House. Although I originally met them at the Caribbean Club in Ilford, we later used the Mocca as our meeting place.

The street gangs in those days consisted of a group of lads whose common bond was a particular sound system. There were lots around: the Kennedy system (to which I belonged), Quaker City, Small Axe, Saxon, Fat Man, King Original, Tubbys and lots of others. It was just like belonging to a football club except that there were fewer members. The music was street reggae. Shaka was my favourite. We didn't like Bob Marley, he was too commercial.

Our reggae was not played on the radio, it was too underground. We made our own hardcore mixes which you get in garage music. Members of a sound system would make dub plates — their own exclusive mix. Every time a dub plate was played in a club, a roar of approval would go up from a section of the crowd. It was a bit like seeing your side score in football. If you annoyed members of another sound system, all hell would break loose. Someone would throw a bottle and the fuse would be lit for all out warfare. There were some serious players out there. For instance, you didn't mess with members of the Small Axe sound. Not if you valued your fingers. They were all armed with tomahawks.

The lasting image I have of Carl Marston is one of classic heroism as he bravely faced his enemy. It was a David and Goliath-style confrontation and reminded me of the Clint Eastwood classic *The Good, the Bad and the Ugly*. Carl was my black knight. He was so impressive I'd put him on a pedestal way above most of our group. The Kennedy posse, to which I belonged, had gone to a packed dance hall in Mile End, east London and were about to leave the club when a massive black guy, who looked nearly 7ft tall, and belonged to another sound system, took a dislike to us.

He challenged Carl. Not with words, but with body language. The two eyed each other up. Carl was my height, about 5ft 10in and nearly a foot shorter than the oaf. He must have been expecting Carl to turn tail and leg it, but Carl just stood there, cigarette dangling from the corner of his mouth like Clint Eastwood. He was calm and intent. He was wearing a long beige coat, the bottom part of which he now swept behind his back with both hands, to reveal an axe.

He kept that pose, looking as if he was about to have a gun fight. His feet, slightly apart, were weighted to the front, ready for action. He would have chopped that hulk to pieces if he so much as moved a muscle against any of us. I'd never seen anything like it in my life. It was better than the movies. The big guy backed down. He knew he'd met his match. I felt proud to be in Carl's company. Afterwards, a massive fight broke out between different groups. Fingers were lost to choppers, and heads were smashed in. I was not to be found anywhere. I'd legged it back home.

Several members of our gang made me cry. They were hard men who could take a lot of punishment as well as giving lots out. I'd go with them to martial arts films late on a Friday night. Afterwards, we'd practise some of the moves. My brother was very fond of the 'claw'. This was used countless times on my head and I'm surprised my hair is intact after the brutal way he scraped my scalp. We'd also jab each other in the solar plexus, the temple and any other vulnerable spot on the body, using the snake, the mantis or the crane. We regarded these movies as classics: *Warriors 2*, *Iron Monkey* and *Snake in the Eagle's Shadow*.

At the same time, I was being taught martial arts, first by Master Kam at the Wu Shu Kwan and then at the Lau-Gar with Neville Ray. But I could still be beaten by other lads. I had a punch-up with David Terriot who was a bit older and bigger than me. He was a hard nut and really hurt me with a blow to my face. I fled home crying. That was nothing, however, compared to what Sledge did to my head with his fist. And one of the Ramsey brothers, huge guys, let me have it whenever I gave them too much lip. It would often be in the form of a hot bag of rice in my face at first, then a hard slap. They all used to beat me up, but by the time I'd reached 15 I said to myself, 'You ain't crying no more.' I'd never run from a one-to-one fight unless the opponent could kill me, but I would leg it from a street situation that looked bad.

Crying over women or relationships is quite different to crying over physical pain. I don't think I'll ever stop tears over personal relationships, particularly when the people involved are very close to me. In terms of physical punishment, however, I have always been able to put up with a lot. Like the time Colin Chambers pulled me up over a wall so that we could sneak into a cinema. He lost his grip and, as his hand slipped past my face, his ring caught my front tooth, twisting it 90 degrees from its original position. Gingerly, he tried pushing it back, but two years later I had to have it removed. Curiously, I felt no great pain.

Perhaps I had been well schooled by my older mates. Bully also seemed impervious to pain. On one occasion he was at a fair with his girlfriend, Linda Rogers, and his money fell under a ride. He knelt down to pick it up and was attacked by a hammer-wielding attendant. The guy was calling him 'black' this, and 'black' that and whacked him with the hammer. Bully took it from him, broke the hammer against an iron railing and then let him have it with his bare fists. He beat the crap out of him. He is one of the most powerful men I know. He'd eat you up and spit you out.

He was extraordinary to watch. He once had a shouting match with Linda at the Mocca Bar and the police were called. They came in a team and Bully sent every one of them flying through the air like rag dolls. It was an amazing sight watching him pick them up, one by one, and tossing them about like an angry child discarding its toys.

When the going got tough in gang fights, I usually stayed away. For some reason, other gangs were always out to get me. Monday nights used to be our club night and we would go down to Ilford Town Hall where I'd won a dance competition. Can you imagine that? I could have been a dancer. I was a right little bopper. Down at Ilford there were a lot of racist whites and we used to fight the skinheads and mods. This particular Monday there was going to be another battle, but it wasn't my cup of tea.

About 200 mods had gathered to fight us. I was sitting in McDonald's waiting for the action when some blokes walked in. I couldn't believe that they were involved. We were mostly young teenagers but these people were in their mid-20s. One sat next to me and said, 'It's a bit fuckin' dark in here.'

He was huge and I thought, Yeah, it sure is. There was no way I wanted to roll around the floor with this grizzly bear. All his mates were coming out of the woodwork. We were surrounded and these guys were not playing around. They'd come tooled up for the occasion. Some had irons and sawn-off shotguns. It could have been very nasty.

Fortunately, I was able to push one of them over and then legged it in the confusion that followed. I think they were after us because, a week earlier, one of our group had smashed a furniture shop window and about ten guys had fallen into a double bed and hammered the life out of another gang member. That time I had stayed around and we had had to fight hordes of people. As we marched down the street like a marauding army, people kept joining our ranks from bus queues and post offices, like volunteers in a wartime emergency.

After one of these sorties, a bottle had been thrown at police who'd chased our gang. We were ordered to stop but as I was the only one who obeyed, they tossed me in the police van and charged me with the offence. I told them I hadn't done anything and on that occasion Dad rightly believed me. He knew I would usually put up my hands if caught.

When I was 15 I was convicted of GBH and threatening behaviour against an Indian guy almost twice my age. I usually went to the Hope Revive pub in Ilford Lane to be with the big boys, although I didn't drink any alcohol. On this particular evening, I was sitting on the pool table and was asked to get off by the man I assaulted. I told him I would if he asked me nicely but he said something derogatory. He must have thought I was a weakling because he was much bigger than me. While verbally abusing me, he also started walking towards me. My brother Dermot was there but didn't have time to intervene.

As the guy approached, I whacked him in the face and it was all over. He was bloodied and beaten and seriously hurt. Bill the barman had, seconds earlier, feared for my safety and armed himself with a monkey wrench to stop the fight, but it was over too soon.

A day later, I was walking down Ilford High Street and about six policemen jumped on me. I thought they were going to do me for nicking but, as I hadn't done anything, I protested, 'Hold on,' I said, 'I ain't nicked nothing yet.' That's when they told me they were holding me for assault. I then saw the Indian guy identifying me and thought, 'What a grass!' Again, my initial fear was that I would be in big trouble with Dad and I begged the police not to call him, but he was already at the police station by the time I arrived.

This time, he supported me. 'Did you win, son?' he asked.

'Yeah, Dad. I knocked him down.'

Dad was pleased. He told the police after they had explained what had happened, 'So he should have done. I would have bashed him up as well. I always told my sons if anyone wants to bash you up, don't let them put you in hospital. But if you steal, then I'll bust you up.' Mum had to pay £30 to the court and I was given 60 hours' community service which took six months to do.

My life wasn't all fighting, though. There was a lot of fun in between and a continual flow of women. Because of my youth, I would like to excuse my behaviour with girls. I would treat them quite badly from time to time because of the influence of the big boys around me. Some of them had been just as tough and cruel to their girlfriends as they were to me. It was part of their macho image. They treated them mean and I followed suit. Women whom you did not love were simply used. We'd never fight over them. We'd just use them and like having them around to do our bidding. Happily, that attitude has long since changed.

I remember going to the Notting Hill Carnival with my friends Colin and Mark Jemott. We got separated and I had no money, although I had arranged with one of my girlfriends to meet her at her house later that night. Her parents were going to be away and I wanted to sleep with her. I didn't want to be embarrassed by boarding a bus without money and getting kicked off, so I walked all the way home. It was a horrendous 15-mile trip. When I finally arrived at her house, it was nearly 4.00am and there was my good friend Mark curled up in bed with her! I was gutted.

I very much regret the way I treated one of my girlfriends. I was inexcusably mean. I used to make her meet me at 1.00am and bring me Kentucky Fried Chicken or fish and chips. She was like a slave to me. I used and abused her and slapped her around. That is not a period I am proud of but I have grown up considerably since then.

Mostly, the girls I went out with were lots of fun. We'd get up to high jinks on the top deck of the number 25 bus and do just about everything except make love. There was one girl I was quite keen on for a few months. I made love to her on Wanstead flats late one night but it turned out to be a horrible experience. We were in the heat of passion when I pushed against the ground with both hands for extra leverage. Instead of feeling *terra firma*, my hand squelched and slid along the grass. I had plonked it smack bang in the middle of a huge mound of dog mess.

Another girlfriend and I were travelling home on the number 25 when the urge to make love overtook me. I couldn't wait to get home so we got off the bus, raced into a derelict house and made passionate love against the crumbling wall. I was exhausted by the end of it because this girl was hefty. She was bigger and heavier than me and the strain really showed. My legs were like jelly. After that I vowed I would do daily leg exercises to build up my muscles.

I left school at 16 not knowing quite what I wanted to do. I went on the dole and continued seeing the boys and having a lot of fun. But I was very hurt at the ending of my close friendship with Colin. When I make friends, I'm very serious about the relationship. Colin had some very fine clothes and gold coins and ducats. They were worth a lot of money and were stolen by one of our circle of friends who then pointed the finger at me. The devastating thing was that Colin believed him.

In the meantime, Mum was becoming increasingly anxious about my friends and the direction, or lack of direction, I was taking in my life. My brother John was already serving in the regular army, serving with the First Battalion, Royal Regiment of Fusiliers in Minden, West Germany. She begged him to persuade me to join. Thank God I did. The decision to do so was a major turning point in my life.

4

FOR QUEEN AND COUNTRY

Platoon Sergeant Weaver was a bastard and a gentleman. He thought he was God. We believed he was and he certainly behaved like a deity. He ruled by fear and scared the living daylights out of me and all the other raw recruits who joined Tobruk Platoon for their initial 18 weeks' training at Bassingbourn Barracks in Royston, Hertfordshire.

Sergeant Weaver was a one-off but I respect him for what he put me through. My first impression was that he was a racist bastard. I was wrong about the 'racist'. He treated everybody the same and put us through the toughest regime I have ever experienced. You would get a pasting just because you were in his platoon. He'd go up to a guy and say, 'Look at those nostrils!' and pull out the man's lip.

To see how tough we were, he'd order us to get down on our knees and stick out our chins. Then he'd walk by and crack jaws with his NCO's baton. It was done to find out if you were a man. There was no racial abuse involved. If you could take it, you were tough and passed the test. In one of our survival practice sessions, I was made to swim under a boat in freezing cold water. Sergeant Weaver watched approvingly as my fellow soldiers then threw me naked into a bed of nettles. While hating him at times, I admired the way Weaver conducted himself. His grooming was immaculate. I had never seen anybody as well turned out as he was.

His approach would pay dividends for us later in our training. When we were sent to Scotland for our final assessment, we were grateful he'd hardened our resolve. That's where they really sorted out the men from the boys. Anyone who put a foot wrong would receive one of several punishments, each more barbaric than the last.

If you were given 'Corporal Rock' as punishment, you were unlucky. It was one of the hardest to endure. You had to carry a big rock on your back for the *whole* day. It was about five stone in weight and, for brief spells, you were made to run with it until you had reached the point of exhaustion. But I would have preferred Corporal Rock to 'Corporal Entrails', which meant wearing a disgusting necklace of raw animal guts and offal for a 24-hour period, even during mealtimes.

While on manoeuvres in Scotland, I escaped the more horrendous punishments but still had to endure an ordeal. I was blindfolded, locked in a corrugated tin shed and then, to brighten the proceedings, a thunder flash used in skirmish attacks was thrown into my 'cell', causing a deafening explosion.

Many of us were given nicknames. At first, I was useless at map reading and my inability to find tracks earned me the nickname 'Pathfinder'.

I went into the Army a boy and came out a man. I was 16 when I enquired at the Forest Gate recruitment centre about becoming a soldier. The wartime slogan 'Your Country Needs You' did not apply to me. *I* needed the *Army*. I missed being with John, and as he was the one who had always pleased my parents, I thought it would be nice to follow in his footsteps, besides which there had been some subtle hints from Mum. I had also seen my brother box in the army finals at Aldershot and thought I'd like some of the action.

Shortly before I approached the recruitment office, John had rung home from Germany to find Mum in tears. She begged him to do her a favour. 'Please, John, for my sake and his, get Nigel to join up, because the way he is going he's heading for prison.' John and Dad worked on me and convinced me to enlist, advising me that it was the best thing I could do.

There was nothing else that interested me at the time so I applied and sailed through the army selection tests before I was 17. Not that they were very hard. You just had to prove you were not too thick by ticking lots of boxes.

Then you were sent away for a couple of days to see how fit you were. After that, there was a delay of several months until I had reached seventeen. I started my training on 11 May 1981. Private Nigel Gregory Benn, Army Service Number 24604617 — a number I will never forget — would soon make his mark. One of the good things about the Army was that you were immediately made to feel part of a new family which had a long history. It gave you a sense of belonging and a provenance which you might not otherwise have had. On top of that, it instilled a sense of direction, comradeship and the guts to carry on when the going got tough. I owe the Army a great deal.

The Royal Regiment of Fusiliers had a proud and distinguished past. Formed in 1968, it was an amalgamation of the Northumberland, Lancashire, Warwickshire and London fusiliers dating back to the seventeenth century. King James II asked Lord Dartmouth to raise a Regiment of Fusiliers at the Tower of London in 1685. They were armed with the snap-hance musket which was the same as the French fusil. The king described his soldiers as 'My Royal Regiment of Fusiliers' and they became the 'Seventh of Foot'.

Their headquarters is still at the Tower, together with regimental memorabilia and silver. Among the documents is a list of my army fights. The records will say I was undefeated.

In 1881, the City of London, in recognition of the regiment and the old trained bands who helped make up its numbers, granted it the treasured privilege of marching through the city with '... drums beating, bands playing, colours flying and bayonets fixed'. I wish I had been there to see the regiment when it took advantage of this privilege on 29 April 1994. That march was held to commemorate the twenty-fifth year of the regiment's formation, but at the time I was away in Barbados.

Immediately prior to joining the Army, I felt I had quietened down a bit. Mum and Dad no longer had problems with school but they were still worried about some of my friends. One or two of the older ones had a bad reputation and had been in trouble with the law. On the odd occasion, I was still a dab hand at shoplifting and had had a run-in with the authorities after stealing from Woolworth's. Apart from that, I was having a high old time, although there was no real direction in my life. While Debbie Hogan was my regular girlfriend, I was still very much into going out with my mates and seeing my older buddies.

My music tastes had also started to change since leaving school. I was into soul music now which meant going to different clubs. Soul clubs were much quieter and more trouble-free than the reggae venues. We went to places like Lacey Ladies in Seven Kings, the 100 Club in Oxford Street, Oscar's and Global Village. Stratford Town Hall and Ilford Town Hall also had good club nights and entry was relatively inexpensive. Our circle of friends included some great dancers with names to match: Shakin'

Stevens, Oily, Mutley and Bassey. We were one big happy family going from club to club.

Debbie and I were far too young for a serious commitment and I was still attracted to other girls, particularly to one with whom I became absolutely besotted. She was the most beautiful black woman I had ever seen. Vanya was a goddess. She had a huge Afro hairstyle, which she sometimes plaited and which seemed to have a life of its own.

We dated but didn't sleep together. Not that I didn't want to. She was gorgeous. I took her back to my mate Paul's one night while his parents were away and sat talking with her for 20 hours. However, by the close of this marathon I was back to where I started. She was far too shy to do anything physical with me at that time.

Later, when we took up again while I was on leave from the Army, our physical relationship flourished. She was as beautiful as ever but less introverted. I don't know why I won her over then, possibly because I was fairly boisterous. She was still a little reticent but a very decent girl. I was proud to be with her.

Bassingbourn Barracks might as well have been in a different country. It seemed a million miles from home. My first night away from Mum was murder. I cried like a baby. For the first time, I realised how vulnerable I still was at 17. What a change from my confident old self. When surrounded by stable and loving parents and family, I had felt tough, invincible and grown up beyond my years. Here at camp I even had a picture of Debbie which I slipped under my pillow and clutched tearfully before going to sleep. Not one of my friends in east London thought I would make it beyond two weeks. They were convinced I would fail to knuckle down to army discipline.

The experience was new to me and it took some time to adapt to the strict regime. It began the moment they woke you. They threw you out of the bed and then turned the bed upside down. But it was not all bad. We had a good bunch of lads and I made friends quickly. Joe Reeves became my best mate in those first six weeks and the other lads in my circle were Ducksy who had been a gardener, Jimmy Henderson, whom we called Jap because of his oriental appearance, Stretch Armstrong who had no teeth, and another Joe who was a massive black guy and a right hard-case.

The training was easy until they tried to get me to map read. We had some free time but in the first weeks there was little or no opportunity of meeting women so I remained faithful to the photograph under my pillow and generally tried to behave myself. I wasn't going to have any old trollop who had been through the British Army, at least not the ones I had seen around Royston.

Once I'd overcome my loneliness and had been given a few days off, I returned to my confident old self again. Feeling happier, Joe Reeves and I became a bit lairy and our antics would sometimes reflect badly on Tobruk Platoon. To teach us a lesson, Sergeant Weaver organised an old ritual which involved running the gauntlet. The whole platoon formed itself into two rows of soldiers and Joe and I had to walk down the aisle between them. The soldiers had been given permission to whack or kick us as hard as they wished. Like a pair of reluctant brides, we began our passage down this dangerous aisle, but it was only poor Joe who suffered an onslaught of blows which rained down on his head, shoulders and back. Nobody dared touch me because I had issued a prior warning that I would beat the hell out of anyone who dared. 'Whack me,' I said, 'and you're marked. Marked!'

Tough as they were, my colleagues had better sense than to attack me. The week before, they had seen me fight a 6ft 9in giant called Pete Driver. He was my first unofficial fight opponent in the Army. Pete was so big, they had to break up two beds to improvise one long enough to accommodate him. We shared the same dormitory and I had been looking out of the window, watching another soldier dismantle a general purpose machine-gun when Pete told me to get down.

Uttering some fairly common expletives, I suggested where he should get off, adding that his size didn't scare me one bit. It seems that he was annoyed with the verbal abuse or else he didn't like my attitude. Either way, the result was the same. He attacked me.

He lurched forward at me like a huge bear and shoved me with the stub of his hand. Thrown back, I recovered and ran at him, knocking him down on to the bed. Then I smacked him in the mouth with my fist and his teeth went through his lip. He was a tough so and so and got up and punched me in the eye. It split and there was blood everywhere. Suddenly, I saw two of him. Two massive bears towering over me. His punch had given me temporary double vision. That was no help whatsoever, just twice as scary! I legged it but the two of him chased after me.

By this time, we had acquired a growing audience and the Sergeant Major, hearing the rumpus, shouted at us to stop. As he did so, I turned around and kicked Pete in his nuts. He didn't budge. It seemed as though he hadn't felt a thing.

Because we shared the same quarters, I was terrified at first that he might throw a wash tub over me while I slept, but he knew the 'koo' — the score. He realised that if he came for me, I wouldn't back down. But, then, I had respect for him, too. He could have inflicted serious damage on me. After that incident we became quite good friends. Pete's height resulted in Sergeant Weaver often making him fall to his knees when talking to him. Gods were not expected to look up at mere privates.

Pride of place on the wall above my brother's head at his barracks in Minden was a photograph of me looking as if I had jumped six feet off the ground while doing a martial arts kick. In fact, the picture lied. I had jumped off a box which was conveniently left out of the shot. However, John had already told his mates and colleagues about my fighting abilities and this picture corroborated his proud boasts, and compounded my reputation even before my arrival in Germany. I was posted to Minden at my request but didn't advise John of the date. I surprised him by springing out from behind a tree in the camp square just as he was returning to quarters from dinner. He was delighted and shocked and hardly recognised me in my flat cap, jeans and trainers.

During the Second World War, our camp had been home to the German SS and a penal battalion. Now it catered for armoured regiments and their personnel carriers which would take us to the Soviet border in the event of attack by the USSR.

The first thing John did on my arrival was to read me the Riot Act. 'You're in the Army, now. Things are going to be slightly different to the way they were back home.'

He stressed that I should keep my temper in check and my hands to myself. Avoid fights at all costs, he warned. I think he was asking me to show tolerance, especially as I would be sharing a room with a real hard nut. Everybody was scared of this guy and John didn't want to see me beaten up.

In spite of the warning, I battered the hell out of the soldier as soon as I moved in. He was playing his music loud, far too loud for my liking and I guessed it was done to get on my nerves or to test my reaction. I asked him to stop and he refused, so I punched the daylights out of him. He tried to have a go at me but I got in first and gave it to him. From that time on, I was one of the main men in camp. Everybody showed respect. John tried once more to read me the Riot Act but his words fell on deaf ears.

You didn't have to be in the Army for very long to realise there were great advantages in being a good sportsman. I was given a work-out in a ring two months into my posting and must have impressed the officers who thought I showed enough promise to continue. John was already in the boxing team training up for a fight. They put me in the ring with Shifty who stood about 6ft 3in and had a massive chest. I panned him all over the ring and the Sergeant Major took me straight out of uniform and into a tracksuit and that was it for the next year or so.

Up until this time, I had had little or no boxing training. I'd been in the ring with John but he had decked me a couple of times and I thought it wasn't for me. Long before this, I'd had a fight with him and he beat the granny out of me. At that time, I was looking for Mum to come and bail me out. John was tough. He may have been more powerful than me but he was not as agile. He was a heavyweight in the Army and only lost two fights, both to the same guy, George Jay. I had to fight Jay because he beat my brother twice and I battered him, even though I had just seen him knock out three other guys.

Curiously, I didn't want to become an army boxer because of my interest in the sport. It was more a matter of personal pride. I wanted to shine and make a name for myself. Perhaps the most pressing reason was being able to get off work and a lot of the unpleasant routines. Being a boxer meant you got special food — steaks instead of slops — and it also meant you could get up at 8.00am instead of 5.45am.

Corporal Jones trained me at first and, as I got better, I began training others. I was constantly excused from army exercises so I could get on with my training, which included running and gym work-outs. When I was doing battalion boxing, Quartermaster Brown and Corporal Mark Gleason trained me. Gleason was a hard man but a good trainer. He still calls me now. Captain O'Grady was the chief man and he made me work really hard. I sometimes resented this but he did the right thing.

Although I thought John would have the edge over me in boxing because he was heavier, he was very wary of my martial arts training. He rightly thought he wouldn't stand a chance because of my speed and power punching. When we sparred, he said he couldn't lay a glove on me. He would tell our mutual friends, 'Nigel would hit me ten times and I was lucky if I could land one punch against him. When I tried, it was too late. He'd already be over the other side of the ring looking at me. I put that down to his martial arts training. His hand speed was phenomenal, absolutely phenomenal.

'When we fought in the Royal Fusiliers, Nigel annihilated the Welsh champion in two rounds. At one stage, he put him against the ropes and gave him 20 punches up and down the body. The Welshman then tried to box and his arm went and it was all over.'

That was some fight. I broke the Welshman's arm with my head. He punched the top of my head in the second round. I nearly blacked out but recovered. I was about 18 then and a welterweight but he was really tough.

When I fought for the battalion against the REME (Royal Electrical and Mechanical Engineers) one of my mates was knocked out. I jumped into the ring and knocked out the guy who did it in a couple of rounds.

John always said my reputation grew at a startling speed and that I was feared in the ring, particularly when we visited Berlin to fight individuals, both as novices and in open-class boxing. The most memorable fight was with the singles winner Harry Harrison of the King's Regiment.

John overheard someone say, 'Watch that guy from the Fusiliers, he is so fast. It will be a very good fight.'

As you can imagine, all the open-class boxers were huddled around the door to watch this fight. The tension was electric as this very good boxer, Harry, had beaten every other person he'd met. But it all changed when I fought him. Harry came into the ring bobbing and weaving about. All of a sudden, I let fly with a left hook, bang, straight on the jaw. Harry hit the middle rope, crashed to the floor and the fight was all over in 17 seconds.

I didn't lose one fight in the Army. The world was my oyster. It was a great feather in my cap to beat these men who had been boxing for years and years.

One fight I remember well was my battle against Corporal Lewis, who was a massive black guy and a real fitness fanatic. He was knocking everybody out like there was no tomorrow. When it came to my turn to fight him, I felt like heading for the closest latrine. I'd seen him in my weight class and he was about 6ft 2in of muscle. He was really, really athletic. You wake up when you see someone like him. As I went for him, I thought, 'Here we go. I'm going to get knocked out for the first time.' But I mullahed him. He may have been four inches taller but I punched him through the ropes and knocked the granny and the grandad out of him. I became an instant hero for wiping the floor with him.

Eventually, I was given the opportunity of fighting at Aldershot in the open-class army championships. Now we were talking about the élite: the Paras, Irish Guards and Green Jackets. I'd made the grade up from novice and I put everything I had into it, winning the championship.

John told me later that Captain O'Grady and the Regimental Quartermaster-Sergeant were going to put money into me when I left the Army. They saw my potential for professional boxing but are still kicking themselves for not having done anything about it. While I was the toast of most of the soldiers and officers in my battalion, there were one or two who were not happy about my achievements. I really hated one officer, whom I was sure loathed the way I had exploited my boxing abilities. There was no love lost between us.

It looked like he had pressed his clothes using a cold mess tin rather than a hot iron. He was a right ex-Sandhurst nob. I would still feel like punching him in the mouth if I met him again now. If we were in a war together, I'd be the first to leave on a jet bound for Barbados.

I could have taken him outside and confronted him in a one-to-one situation with no witnesses present. He irritated me to such an extent that I still feel hatred for him. Our CO, on the other hand, was posh but very nice. And there was another NCO in charge of us, Lieutenant Keegan, who was a lot smoother.

I have already described how my sex life began at a very young age and that I had been a selfish lover, more interested in satisfying myself and ignoring the techniques necessary for a mutually pleasurable event. This all changed in Germany. The country proved to be a great teacher, particularly its fräuleins.

Not long after I was posted to Minden, I met a German woman who was much older than me. It was at Snoopy's nightclub in Bielefeld. I was dressed like a 'sticksboy' which was the black fashion then. We liked gold sovereigns, gold ducats on long chains and brim hats. I had a massive ducat, suede shoes and a jacket with an open-neck shirt underneath. She had the hots for me although she was there with another man. She was short with dark hair and a good body. I preferred dark-haired women, although my fiancée, Mary, whom I loved to distraction and lived with when I left the Army, was blonde.

She came over after I'd gone to the bar and asked for a

dance when the reggae came on. Me? I looked around. Apart from John, I was the only black brother there. I didn't believe this was happening to me. I was still a kid in Germany. I hadn't even talked to a woman up to that point and this lady had a male friend in tow! Everybody was staring at us. She took me to the dance floor and held me so tightly that penetration was the only way we could have got closer. In her lifetime, the woman, who was 31, must have had more pricks than a second-hand dartboard, but I wasn't to know that at the time. She whispered in my ear. She said how much she would like to take me to a restaurant. As she danced, she moved her head from side to side. I had to keep ducking in case I connected with her parrot nose.

The meal she had promised was delicious. She drank a toast to me with neat gin. Then another, followed by a third. I was reeling. After that we got stuck into the main course, duck à l'orange. She'd ordered plenty of German wine and after our fresh fruit cake, she ordered brandy. I knew I would have to work hard for the meal. I suggested we cut it short and went back to her place. She stripped me, went to the bathroom and returned naked. I gave it to her and she was dying for it. She had a lovely bed with a full-length mirror along the wall. I saw our reflected bodies and thought: 'This 17-year-old boy is doing good.'

By now, she was really making me earn my meal. She wanted more and more and more. I was Lester Piggot riding Red Rum. I was exhausted after doing it the second time. Her whole body shuddered and I fell asleep on her heaving breasts. Half-way through the night, I felt her hand working its way down my back to my bottom. I woke with a jerk as she tried to push her finger into my anus.

'Hey,' I said. 'You leave my black ass alone. Ain't nobody touching my backside. I'm not that kinky. I'm not a homosexual.'

I managed a third time but couldn't go the fourth, no matter what she did, and that lady was experienced! She taught me a lot. In the morning, we were woken by her young daughter who brought us a cup of tea. This was too much for me. I didn't even realise she had been married. I returned, bleary-eyed, to camp. My clothes were in disarray and I begged John to look after me. 'I can't take any more,' I pleaded. That was the first time he had heard me admit defeat.

She wanted me back but I managed to avoid her by concentrating on two other German girls called Anke and Gabrielle, both of whom became my girlfriends. Anke was my age, and Gabrielle about six years older. I met Anke at a disco and she was stunning. Her body was fitter than mine. She had her own business. Gabby was beautiful in a different way. She had long hair down to her bottom, a slim body with small breasts and quite big hips. I met her at a field sports day. She had been married to an English serviceman and had a kid, so I thought I had quite a good chance. That's a joke, but I chatted her up and she and Anke, while both unaware of it, became my main girlfriends, although I had to do a bit of nifty juggling to make sure the girls didn't find out that I was two-timing them.

Apart from them, I had a considerable number of one-night stands, some of which were quite eventful. The German girls I met seemed to be fairly uninhibited. They didn't seem to have the normal hang-ups about making love on the first night. In fact, they often suggested it!

Sometimes I wish I'd been more choosy, but then youth can be excused many things. I still shudder a little at the memory of making love to John Lennon. Not the Beatle, but a German girl we called by that name because of her looks. While she was a lot of fun to be with, her looks ensured that you could safely leave her with your mates and know she'd still be there waiting on your return. However, after a stiff drink or three, this girl became Marilyn Monroe. We went out into the fields together and, like a gentleman, I removed my jacket and laid it on the ground before undressing her and making love. Fired with passion, I had not noticed how wet the ground had been and, when we returned, virtually the whole camp had a laugh at my expense. Everyone took the mickey.

'Oh mate, you didn't go with her, did you?' they asked incredulously. I denied it. I lied and lied but the evidence was on the back of my muddied blazer. It was the first time my fellow soldiers had seen a black man turn red.

When we were given home leave, I would return to the clubs I'd visited with my mates before joining the Army and meet some new girlfriends. My relationship with Debbie had started to fizzle out and I had met Vanya whom I really liked. I'd also started a relationship with another girl called Julie Laurent, a really pretty black girl in her 20s. Understandably, I became quite emotional when, after returning from leave on one occasion, I received a call from her ending our relationship. I was so upset that I called up my mate Dave Barnett and drank a full bottle of Malibu in the record time of eight minutes. My brother John tried to cheer me up after finding me on all fours in the street. He picked me up by the scruff of the neck and hauled me towards his car, and its giggling passengers. He had been looking forward to a night out with some girls who worked in a bar, but just before I was thrown on to the back seat, the potent mixture of Malibu and curry combined to make me let rip a loud fart, after which I fell asleep. What had been a bit of fun for the girls had now become rather more unsavoury, so they really went off me in a big way.

While in the Army, I considerably increased the scar tissue on my body through playing rugby. I received a particularly bad wound to the inside of my knee where flesh was ripped out, leaving a gaping hole and white skin. After it had healed, I lost some of the feeling, particularly where the skin had formed a thin white scar along my leg. However, I was able to use this to my advantage whenever I wanted to avoid rigorous field exercises. I used to poke the scar with a knife and then I was able to cut it with a razor blade without feeling a thing.

We once went away for exercises to another part of Germany, a horrible place where all we did was dig trenches and train solidly for two weeks. I was depressed about it and told John I was getting off these exercises. With that, I jumped into one of the ditches and slit open my wound again, pretending a rock had caused the injury. With blood gushing from my self-inflicted wound, they took me back to camp and I was as cheerful as anything. I lived the life of Riley, sneaking women back to my quarters while the other chaps were slogging away in ditches.

Even when I was meant to be in serious training for an army boxing match, I would be out with the girls having a drink. I didn't win them all, though. John and I missed out badly on two girls we fancied. We'd seen them at one of the bars in Bielefeld and they were our fantasy figures. They used to look at us and we at them and one day we were about to make a move when they were surrounded by about 30 friends. As they looked a bit Italian we thought we'd better not mess with them in case of Mafia involvement.

I was very lucky not to have been court-martialled after I'd been out on escape evasion field exercises in Westphalia. These exercises were treated as being very important for survival in war. We would be dropped off about 100 miles from camp, given a minimum amount of money, just a few Marks to phone base in case of dire emergency, and told to live off the land and make our way back to camp. Soon after we set off, helicopters and Rottweiler dogs would begin to follow our trail. I was paired with George Barry, a mate of mine, and we set off together in the foulest weather imaginable. All we had for warmth was one blanket and on the first night we slept in a field. We begged a German family for food and they gave it to us. We were meant to live off potatoes and carrots and the like but after a second night in a stable covered with cow dung which, by morning, had frozen to my body, I'd had enough.

I telephoned my girlfriend Anke and told her to pick us up. She told us to hitch-hike to Bielefeld and she'd collect us from there. For the rest of the exercise, I slept with a beautiful German girl between silk sheets, had hot baths every night and was fed the best food and wine. This was the life. When it was time to return to base, we asked the girls to drop us off about 20 miles away so we'd look at least a little genuine after our 'rough' ordeal. Knowing how serious a court-martial could be, we memorised the story we'd give and the places where we had slept rough.

One of the officers interrogated us desperately, hoping we'd crack. He knew we hadn't walked back but couldn't prove it. We stuck to our guns and wouldn't change our story. To his dismay, we got away with it.

While I was in Germany, I had several fights with other soldiers but avoided getting into serious trouble because of my sporting skills. On one occasion, I was at 7 Platoon in Elizabeth Barracks when a 6ft 5in squaddie stumbled his way down the corridor asking for John Benn. He was a bit drunk and had a plaster over his hand. Nobody was going to try to damage any member of my family so I went up to him and gave him a football kick in the mouth. He dropped to his knees and I tried to break his neck. John, whose room was on the top floor of the building, would have punched him down to 1 Platoon but I wasn't going to let this guy near my brother. I could sense his hostility and, without asking questions, let him have it. The next day he said to me that I'd beaten him only because he was drunk. I asked him if he wanted to have another go and he cried off. Big as he was, I had to stand my ground, although if he'd whacked me while he was sober, he would probably have knocked me out.

My most serious fight was with another soldier, a Green Jacket, and the events leading up to it took place over the period of a week. Our boys were being beaten up badly by the Green Jackets. They were all London boys who fought in packs and any time one of the Fusiliers went downtown, they'd be set upon. My mate Jacko had been savaged by a guy with red hair and when we heard about it we decided this bullying had to end. A posse of us, about 20 guys, went downtown looking for the redhead. We had two men spread out along the road for about a mile to Red Fred's where the Green Jackets used to drink. It had been our pub before that. With the other men scattered about I went in with Bic and Cockney Jacko and asked him to point out the guy who'd beaten him up. He wasn't there so we challenged some of his mates who were drinking. They refused so we went outside and waited.

We hoped Jacko's assailant might show and after some time a couple of soldiers came down by themselves. I asked them if they were Green Jackets and when they replied positively, that was it. Boom! I lashed into them and knocked out one of the guy's teeth. By the end of the fight he lay demolished. He had to have 14 external stitches and 7 internal ones. During the fight, Bic jumped up really high and came crashing down on his knee on this guy's head.

Afterwards, there was a big inquiry and the military police were called in to investigate. A description had been given that one of our men, a big black guy wearing an Arsenal sweatshirt, had laid into the Green Jacket. Everybody thought it was Dave Barnett who was twice my size. I was quite thin and small at the time. The police started hassling Dave quite a bit so I put my hands up to it. They were not going to court-martial a boxing champ. I only got 14 days' loss of privileges. In a way, we had been like Tottenham fans going out to get Arsenal fans, but the Green Jackets deserved our revenge.

5

FIRST THE GOOD NEWS

The Commanding Officer, Royal Regiment of Fusiliers, was to make an announcement to the assembled battalion. About time. It was December 1983 and we'd been waiting months for confirmation of the good news we hoped to hear. Rumours had spread like wildfire that the first and second battalion would be getting a plum posting in Cyprus. That meant loads of sunshine, beaches and white sands, not to mention bikini-clad girls on holiday.

'There's good news and bad news,' Colonel Robinson began. 'I expect you will want to hear the good news first.' Without waiting for a reply, he continued, 'You have been expecting a posting in Cyprus and I am happy to say that ...' The troops hollered and cheered. Confirmation at last! The CO went on, 'I am happy to say that we will be going to Cyprus.' We went wild. 'But here's the bad news. Before we go to Cyprus, we are going to Ballykelly in Northern Ireland for two years from next January.'

There was stunned silence. This was typical of the way bureaucracy worked in the Army. Deeply disappointed, half the soldiers didn't bother returning to their barracks after assembly. They headed for the nearest bar to drown their sorrows. Nobody in their right mind wanted to serve in Ireland. Especially this boy. I mean, how many black Paddys had anyone seen on the streets of Belfast?

I didn't want to go there. Get shot up for what? It was somebody else's war, not mine. It had nothing to do with me. The IRA are much more deadly and powerful than the Mafia. I still regard them with respect and fear. I've been threatened in the past and that's one lot you don't mess with.

But if it happens, it happens. There is very little you can do about it. Three of my mates were blown to pieces on an innocent fishing trip during a few days' leave. One of them could only be identified by a ring he was wearing. The victims had held no grudge against the Irish. All of them were simply doing their job without malice or hatred. Their widows will have to live with this tragedy for the rest of their lives. It pains me to think about it.

I have no quarrel with the Irish. In fact, I prefer some of them to the English. Unfortunately, many people make the mistake of associating the IRA with the Irish people and that is not the case at all.

Once our regiment had established itself in Ballykelly, it was not at all bad living over there. It was certainly a hard lesson and we were on edge much of the time, but I managed to avoid taking part in the more deadly wargames which some of my colleagues went in for.

Before we were transported, there was still much to do in Germany. I had to sort out various relationships as well as repay personal debts. Anke was deeply in love and had given me a diamond ring as a token of her affection. My dad now wears it. I was very attached to Anke and told her I would be back. That was the least painful way to leave her.

On the debit side, there was my colleague's smashed up BMW. It had been a brand-new car before I wrote it off. I crashed it while he was away on leave and had to find enough cash to pay him back. He was on holiday and I had agreed to buy the car on his return, but I was too impatient to wait for him to come back so I let myself into his room and found the keys to his BMW. Unfortunately, I hadn't passed my test at the time and my driving skills were woefully inadequate for a high-performance car. Furthermore, the weather had been atrocious. Continual rain on the cobbled stone roads around the camp had made conditions extremely dangerous. The cobbles were as slippery as ice.

One of my friends had tried teaching me the basics of advanced motoring. I hope he kept away from driving schools on his return to civilian life. He showed me handbrake turns and other stunts which a learner shouldn't even think about. Now I was in the driving seat, feeling for the first time the power I could muster at the touch of a few controls. The urge to put my foot down was far greater than the need to obey speed limits and soon I was gliding around camp, delirious with joy, like a kid who'd just got his first Christmas present. However, the combination of speed and slippery cobble stones spelt disaster. I lost control and found myself skidding towards a kerb which I hit full on. The car bounced over the pavement and smacked into a tree which it uprooted. My hands gripping the steering wheel, I hung on with lip-biting determination, bewildered by the slow-motion destruction taking place and hoping against hope that it was all a bad dream.

But the dream had not yet ended and the car continued its journey of demolition, crashing into a NAAFI building and then catapulting through a wall into the bedroom of the lady who ran it. Shaking, but relieved that I had come to no harm, I switched off the engine and wrenched open the doors to inspect the trail of this man-made hurricane. Had the NAAFI manageress been in bed at the time of impact, there is little doubt that she would have been killed. I couldn't believe the damage. Although the car was a write-off, it took one hell of a battering and it made sure it damaged itself before it damaged me. I was in deep shit, let me tell you. In fact, I'd never been in so much potential trouble in the Army before. Happily, however, after some fancy footwork, I somehow managed to wriggle out of having to pay for the damaged building and the matter was quietly dropped.

Compared to me, my brother John was a saint in the Army, just as he had been at home. I was always getting into trouble, although the complaints were mostly trivial. I think I had more charges brought against me in a week than my brother had in his six years. Violations of the rules were normally punished by way of fines. There were fines for losing working parts of a gun and fines for insubordination. I lost quite a bit of money this way.

One of the NCOs given the task of collecting these fines was too frightened to ask me. He had been given the job of collecting barrack damages. When you hand over your block to the next regiment, damages sustained to the barracks must be paid every month. He had noted a deduction of about 20 Marks but was terrified of my reputation as a fighter and asked John to collect the outstanding dues.

Ever since I had been posted to Germany, John had played the role of the protective older brother. In fact, he signed up for another three years just to make sure he would be around with me and was quite annoyed when I left before he did.

My final confrontation outside the boxing ring took place on the streets of Bielefeld when two Germans tried to mug me. I was walking along a quiet road when I noticed two guys strolling down towards me and then separate as I came close. Their intention was for me to walk between them, at which point they would attack from each side. The taller of the two went for me first but he was not fast enough. I cracked him on the jaw and he fell down like a lead weight. The other panicked and legged it.

By the time I was ready for the transfer to Ballykelly, I'd fallen deeply in love with Mary Nichols. I had never felt so much passion for any other girl, apart from my first love Susan Marsh. By coincidence, Susan had married an American and was living in Frankfurt during my posting in Germany. She was now a mother of two children and John and I had been invited to visit her. The ten-hour return journey by car was an eye-opener but disappointing. I couldn't believe the change in her. I was barely out of my teens, a carefree boy with an image of a girl who would be exactly like me.

That image was permanently shattered. Instead of the young girl I had known, I saw a mum with kids and a husband.

Now my thoughts were only for Mary. I had courted her during my leave and was seriously in love. Although we had never been mates, I was at school with her brother Joe who did a huge double-take when he found me comfortably ensconced in an easy chair in his parents' sitting room. He remembered me as the school bully and, as such, I was the last person you would bring home to meet your mum, dad and sister. However, they were easy to get along with and his sister was in love with me so I was accepted without question.

Mary was two or three years younger than me. I had first set eyes on her at Valentine's Park in Ilford. We would walk past each other in our own group of friends, exchanging shy and secretive looks. We kept this up for some time, aware of the attraction but too nervous to do anything about it. Some months later, we crossed paths again at the Palais, a club in Ilford, and this time we summoned up enough courage to talk.

Mary was blonde and very good looking. I still remember the clothes she wore on our first date — a green canvas jacket and faded blue jeans. She looked like Goldie Hawn in the film *Private Benjamin*. She was really beautiful, with a face that reminded me a little of the actress Felicity Kendall. Eventually, we became lovers and she was my first fiancée. We had a really good relationship which didn't just depend on sex. There was more love than lust. She would write to me every week. Her letters were like treasures arriving in the post.

We had so much going for us. Her family was lovely. Her dad, Fred, and mum, Patricia, welcomed me into their home and their hearts and I was besotted with their daughter. I always liked women with whom you could have a laugh and Mary had a great sense of humour. She would copy the antics of my brother Mark and have us in fits of laughter. Her dad even got my father trying Indian food, which he normally wouldn't eat.

The camp at Ballykelly was 13 miles from Londonderry but it was nearly eight months before I ventured outside its perimeters. I continued boxing but occasionally had to take part in army exercises and operations. It was an education being there and I was continually aware of the threats facing us. But let me tell you, I was not going to be a foolhardy volunteer and stick out my neck for inclusion on dangerous missions. One of the great lessons I had learned from the streets of east London was survival.

My knee wound from Germany had healed up pretty well by now so I could no longer slash open the same scar to get off exercises. However, I became aware of other convenient foot problems, like verrucas and ingrowing toenails, and these provided sufficient relief from boring drudgery in the field.

The danger money they paid us in Northern Ireland was a joke. It was about £2.50 a day — a hell of an incentive to get blown up for Queen and country. I would look at some of the wet-behind-the-ears 19-year-olds who were meant to back me up on manoeuvres and think, 'No way!' I was not mad enough to put my trust and life in the hands of young kids who could hardly feed themselves. There was also the constant reminder at the back of my mind, saying, 'This isn't your war.'

Mum was always worried about me being in Northern Ireland. Dad told me, 'She hates it, Nigel. Mum is trembling and scared. She fears for you and John.' Dad reckons that being in the Army and serving in Northern Ireland changed my whole attitude to life. He said it gave me discipline and direction, although he was aware that I didn't like being there.

Once you've been there you're not scared of what anybody can do to you. We were required to undertake guard and patrol duties near the border in what was bandit country and that was a bit hairy. You could be blown up or shot at by a sniper. I have never fired a shot in anger, neither was one ever fired at me but, then, I kept out of the firing line as much as possible. Nevertheless, there was always the danger of being killed and we lost a total of five blokes on two tours. One soldier was shot twice through the head and then there was the terrible bomb blast which killed three of my mates in a van at Enniskillen. The explosion was so devastating that the Army wouldn't ask the wives to identify the soldiers' remains.

Because of the advantages it gave, boxing continued to be the most important thing to me. I still hadn't conformed but a little eccentricity was allowed in sportsmen. Besides this, my reputation was growing all the time because I had never lost a fight. John was more than a little surprised at what they allowed me to get away with, and he liked relating my escapades to family and friends.

'Nigel was away on patrol with Z Company for a

month and I was back at the main base in Ballykelly. All of a sudden your brother is back. I see this guy with boxing boots, denims, combat jacket and a Russian furry hat with a red star on it! That's how he dressed for the four weeks they were down there. We were howling with laughter. He was the only one who could get away with that. It was obviously because of his boxing skills. They brought a guy from Queen's Regiment to fight him. This soldier was an old hand in the ring. He'd had 60 fights. Nigel took him out in the first round.'

While it was mostly my brother who battled for me, I was determined to seek revenge on someone who had beaten him in a boxing fight. George Jay was my final boxing opponent in the Army. Some time earlier he had beaten John and I said that before I left, I wanted to fight him, not through hate but just to even the score. He was a heavyweight while I was only a middleweight, but I beat him on points. Family honour was restored.

A few people asked me if I would consider taking up fighting professionally but that was the last thing to enter my mind. I only saw it as a means to an end while serving with the Fusiliers. It made life easy. I was better fed, excused from boring exercises and enjoyed a new status as the regimental star.

The cushiest number I ever had in the Army was when I became an RP (regimental policeman).

The camp nick was always full. When I was there it was empty. I'd give them a hard time and enjoy it. A squaddie's idea of a good night out was 15 pints of beer and a good scrap, but they knew if they went to jail with me in charge, they'd get mauled. Some of the men would go really wild. We had a Geordie battalion and some of them lived for drink. One drop of Newcastle Brown and they'd be anybody's. It took me a while to understand their accent but I really got on with those guys, much

Main Picture: Mr and Mrs Benn.
Inset: A scary bungee jump with my wife Carolyne.

Top: Giving it to Vincenzo Nardiello.
Bottom: Me making an entrance before my fight with Danny Perez.

My fights with Chris Eubank have become almost legendary, and our rivalry one of the most famous in boxing. But he managed to surprise me the day I met him at the Brit Awards ...

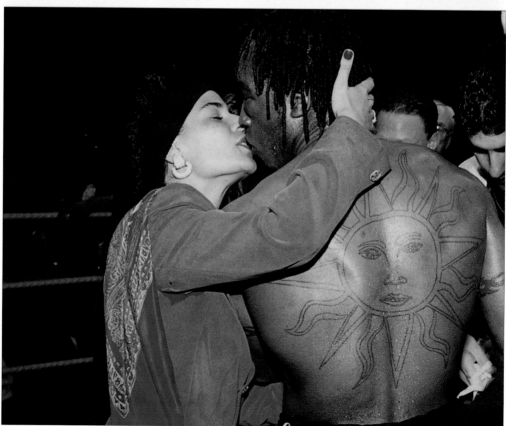

After McClellan, the fight game wasn't the same anymore. I lost my title to Sugar Boy Malinga in 1996, but I gained something more precious that day, when Carolyne agreed to be my wife. This picture also shows the sun tattoo I had done in LA.

Top: Boxing's not my only sporting love. Here I am with Robbie Williams at Wembley.
Inset: Now that my boxing career is over, I have time to relax with Carolyne.

Marvin Hagler is one of my inspirations. Here I am with him in France.

Top: With Michael Watson in 1989. Michael was a good friend, and I was happy to be able to help him after his disastrous fight with Chris Eubank. We don't speak now though, since Michael accused me of doing coke.
Bottom: Mixing it at the Forum in London for the International Dance Music Awards.

The ref stopped my fight against Mauro Galvano in the third round, and I took home the WBC super-middleweight belt.

better than with the Cockneys.

I happily confess to the fact that I enjoyed bashing blokes about if they got in trouble. It was a great power kick and also the only way to win their respect and keep the jails empty. I'd make them mark time with a heavy artillery Wombat shell. I told one soldier who was particularly lairy to stand against a wall while holding the shell in both hands and then gradually squat down, kicking out his legs in turn. Once he was down, I cracked a broom handle across his legs.

I really used to give it to them. I had power. If people hated me for it, I didn't care. I knew I was getting out of the Army soon. When they were under my control, the detainees had to march to dinner with me and I would make them perform mundane tasks like picking up litter. When the RSM wasn't in camp, I was in charge and that felt really great.

The job itself was a doddle. As the RP you only had to keep order in camp, so there was lots of free time and you were excused from normal duties and exercises which other soldiers had to do. I was also able to sneak women into my bedroom because now I was in the privileged position of having a room to myself and not having to share with other squaddies. Furthermore, there was nobody to arrest me unless I did something seriously wrong.

For about six months of my posting, I had an Irish girlfriend called Karen. She was a fiery lass, the way I liked them. I met her at a camp disco but hadn't realised until I became an RP that all women allowed in camp had to be vetted. Some of them had been around for nearly ten years and we had all sorts of nicknames for some of these old pot-boilers. One group from Coleraine were known as the Coleraine Commandos. They used to think I looked like Leroy from *Fame*. Karen was nice looking but some of them, well, you had to be really under the weather or pull a sack over their head before you did anything. Fortunately, I could break the rules and my social life flourished.

However, there was another side to socialising with women, a much more dangerous and sinister aspect. Vetting was not just a formality but an essential safeguard. There had been a number of instances where women had lured soldiers off base and then left them to the mercy of IRA killers. I could have been a victim myself. On one date, I met a girl off base and suddenly broke into a sweat, thinking, 'What am I doing? I don't know this girl at all. I know nothing of her background. Am I being set up?' I walked away from our tryst. You just never knew.

It's always the silly things that catch you out in life. While I avoided detection when sneaking women into my room, I was unceremoniously 'sacked' from my cushy number over a daft prank. I 'borrowed' a pair of military handcuffs and took them out of camp on a visit to England. On arrival at Heathrow Airport, I chained my mate to some railings. I don't know why I did it, for a laugh I guess. He was locked up in the pouring rain and left there for an hour, while I toured the periphery roads.

The story of this dastardly deed got back to camp fairly quickly — in fact, all was revealed before my return. The RSM, who is God when it comes to anything like this, ordered an inventory to be taken. If anything is missing you answer to him and if it can't be accounted for, ass gets kicked. My brother John telephoned me in London and I was ordered to return the handcuffs immediately. On my return, I was relieved of my duties as an RP and sent back to Z Company.

I left the Army in January 1985 with some misgivings and an excellent reference. I'd served four years and 265 days. The CO personally gave me a glowing report. He said I had been a fine soldier and that I had excelled in the field of sport. He described me as a natural athlete, good at rugby and boxing and said my conduct had been exemplary. I had good motivation and was an asset to the regiment. My departure, he emphasised at the bottom of the reference, would be a sad loss to the battalion. His words of praise, which most of my friends thought applied to somebody else, worked a treat in getting me a job in a security firm.

I came out of the Army a man. In spite of that, there were problems adjusting to civilian life. At first I went back to Mum and Dad's to sort things out and decide what I wanted do. But civvy life was not what I expected and I became depressed. While it had been good leaving the Army, I wasn't aware of the tremendous impact it had made on me. After all, I had spent nearly a quarter of my life as a soldier.

I had never wanted to make the Army a career but it was difficult leaving my mates and the security of the regiment. All of a sudden, I was deprived of the comradeship of guys who'd been around me for almost five years. I was on my own. It was going to be difficult taking that big step back to suburbia.

Habits die hard. With my training in Northern Ireland etched into my memory, I was always up and alert early in the morning. It took me about three months to come back down to some form of normality. Every morning I would be checking my car, feeling under the wheel arches, looking everywhere. In fact, I am still in the habit of doing this. Even now I keep alert in case someone is following me and I still observe precautions like not stopping too close to another car, to allow enough room to drive off in the event of an emergency.

Although the Army offered a good life and very good experience, I needed something else. However successful my boxing career had been, I had no plans to continue fighting after I left. It had served a very useful purpose and that was now at an end.

The best consolation prize for me after leaving the Army was returning to Mary. We could now be together on a permanent basis. We moved into a flat in Stanley Road, Ilford. I got engaged to her at 21 but both parents were against us committing ourselves at such a young age. She was intelligent and fun to be with, although we would argue over stupid things. While living with Mary, I suffered from my enduring problem — my inability to keep my dick in my pants. I was still partying and trying to find girls without realising I already had the best girl on the planet.

My love affair with uniforms had not ended. I simply exchanged my army fatigues for the regulation grey of a security company. One of the first sites I guarded was a green field at Roding in Redbridge. It was being developed into Roding Hospital. I never believed that, years later, I would be going there for private treatment after defending my WBC super-middleweight title against Henry Wharton. The hours I worked there were long and tedious, up to 15 hours a day.

At Redbridge, various checkpoints were positioned around the site and I had to walk to each of them at given times during my shift and clock-on with a key. As a short-cut, I ripped off all the checkpoints from their posts, labelled them and then clocked on, one after the other without having to walk around. Having done that, I suddenly came to the worrying conclusion that I needed to be Speedy Gonzales and faster than Superman to have done the rounds so quickly. Fortunately, my clocking-on had not registered the time and I got away with it, unlike my friend who was caught half asleep with his feet up on the table and wearing no uniform. He was instantly sacked.

There was no shortage of security work for someone who had served in Northern Ireland and I kept changing jobs in the hope of finding one that I would really like. The only job I got turned down for was at Liberty's in the West End of London.

For several weeks I worked as a store detective at Woolworth's in their Dalston branch and made the terrible mistake of accusing an innocent man of shoplifting. I saw a guy put what I thought was an object in his shoe. I'd been watching him for a long time because his actions had aroused my suspicion. But when I had apprehended him, the terrible truth dawned on me that I'd made a mistake. He was rightly furious.

'You're a blood brother, man,' he protested. 'No, I never took nothing. I could take you to court, man. What the fuck are you doing?' I felt really bad and wondered what the hell was I doing. But then everyone can make mistakes.

Working long and staggered shifts took its toll on me. I was always knackered, always falling asleep and matters were coming to a head with Mary. We were quarrelling too much and too often. Sometimes I came home dog tired at 8.00am. Mary had been studying for an economics degree and our lifestyle was being messed up by the hours I worked. I was getting cheesed off with my job and my life. After the Army, I wanted some red-carpet treatment, not to be part of a slave labour brigade. I also decided that I would not be making a career in security. I had enjoyed being back in uniform, it felt like being back in the Army, but the last thing I wanted was to be a security guard for the rest of my life and have nothing to show for it.

With all this going on and my insecurities regarding Mary becoming worse, I reached a turning point in my life. It came about as a result of a security van being short of a guard. I was asked to stand in. That meant riding in the back of an armoured transit van with responsibility for over £^{1}/2 million in cash. Can you imagine the temptation of sitting on that amount of loot while being paid peanuts and realising that you would never amass such a fortune guarding it? I thought 'Oh, mate, I really need this, don't I?' I could feel it. 'Look at this lovely money. God, wouldn't I like it to be my money. Should I try to take it?'

A little bit of rationalisation crept in as I toyed with the thought of acquiring this fortune. The money was bound to be insured so who would I be hurting? Certainly not the security firm, nor the people for whom it was destined. So why not?

I had a mate who knew all about these things. If I needed anybody to help me it would be him. With that, I began working on my blueprint for robbing the security van of £^{1}/2 million.

At that time, I owned a beige Triumph car and used it for doing a recce of the van's journey. I knew that the van driver would not be informed of his route until he was about to set off with the money. That procedure was introduced to make it difficult for an insider to tip off accomplices planning to rob the vehicle. Obviously, I wasn't the first to be tempted.

My role in this robbery would be to pass over the money after a gun was held to my head. I had friends who could provide us with shooters so that was no problem either. By the time I had everything lined up to execute the plan, however, I began to have second thoughts. All the brainwashing from Dad about being honest and leading a decent life started to nag at me. On the other hand, everything had been prepared for me to go ahead with the plan and, with luck, live the life of Riley after its successful completion. But what if it all went wrong? Eight to ten years behind bars would take away my youth for ever. And what about Mary?

I bottled out. When it came to doing it and everything was in place — I had only to name the date — I couldn't go through with it. This was not how I wanted to live my life. I decided then that I wanted to make an honest living. I didn't want a criminal record. My parents wanted to be proud of me and I did not want to disappoint them. That's what they had strived for all their lives and one moment of madness like this could have ruined everything.

That still left me with a problem. I did not want to continue with the long hours and little pay as a security guard. My life was going nowhere. The urge to do something different was bringing me closer to my destiny — fighting. West Ham boxing club beckoned but before I became seriously involved as an amateur, I took part in a prize fight at Lacy Ladies in Seven Kings, east London, which I used to think was the best soul club in England.

I had never been to a prize fight before, nor had it ever occurred to me to attempt prize fighting. My opponent was a guy called Lloyd who thought he was the English version of Marvin Hagler. Wrong — I was! The purse was £150, the biggest I had ever got. People used to go there to settle their differences. I had gone there only to watch but then thought it might be a good way to earn some cash. Lloyd was their local boy and had already dispatched several challengers. 'Any more challengers?' he asked cockily.

Lloyd was in his late 30s and when I stepped into the makeshift ring, wearing just my jeans, he told me he was going to beat me up. I had nothing to lose and he didn't frighten me but he tried to laugh at me. He had seen big guys come and go and gave me lots of mouth. The audience were busily exchanging bets — some were actually backing me — or watching Lloyd attempt a psychological victory before punching me to the ground, or so he thought. I murdered him. I did two rounds with him and knocked him out. He said I was lucky. I said, 'Ta-ta,' took the money and left.

6

LOST GOLD

West Ham Amateur Boxing Club in east London was a famous breeding ground for boxers. Loads of the big names came from that stable, including my trainer Jimmy Tibbs. I first went there for social reasons when I was still living with Mary. Roy Andre was my sparring partner and Mark Kaylor, the British and Commonwealth Middleweight champion whom Jimmy had trained, had just left. It was probably one of the best amateur boxing clubs around at the time. It had produced people like Terry Spinks (British Featherweight Champion and Olympic Gold Medallist), Ron Barton (British Light Heavyweight Champion), and Billy Walker.

When I joined, I had to see Dave Woodward and was put into the ring to show the club members what I could do. I said nothing about my army experience, letting them decide if I was good enough. I enjoyed watching them try to figure me out. There was no doubt they were impressed with my performance but you could see them thinking they had a rough diamond here.

Dave Woodward became my trainer but although I only wanted to fight on an amateur basis, everything was leading up to me becoming professional. Not least because I was beating everybody I fought.

Against club predictions, I beat my sparring partner Roy Andre. He had knocked me down once during the fight, blacking me out — the only time it had ever happened to me. But I got up again and everyone thought I had slipped. Sure I slipped, on to his right hand! From there I put everything I had into the fight and stopped him in the second or third round.

My most traumatic fight in amateur boxing was against Rod Douglas. That was the first time I had ever lost a fight. He was a really powerful guy and we punched each other from pillar to post. When he beat me, I cried my eyes out for a year. I couldn't handle defeat, not after my record.

Although I had lost on points against Douglas, I considered myself the better fighter. Both of us had been on the amateur circuit and had won all our other fights. I had to make 10st 6lb which was a pretty hard thing to do. Sometimes all you could eat at night was a lemon to drain you out. Rod Douglas was the more experienced boxer and I felt there was some favouritism shown towards him. However, that didn't lessen the depression I felt at losing. Like me, he came from the East End of London but he had been fighting as an amateur since he was 13.

After the fight, I was quite sore and felt like giving in. If I couldn't beat him there was not much point in carrying on. I was in such bad shape I couldn't even eat properly. Soon after the fight, Mary bought us some fish and chips but the inside of my mouth was all cut up and my tongue was slit at both sides. Each time I tried to eat chips, salt entered my wounds and trying to eat became unbearable. All I could do was gingerly roll some of the food around in my mouth.

For a whole year, my brother Dermot mercilessly needled me about losing the fight. He even called me Rod. 'Go on, Rod,' he would say, trying to wind me up further. Losing to Rod Douglas was so devastating that it nearly spelt the end of my boxing career. I wanted to retire. That was it. I never wanted to box again. Then, because of all the riling from Mark, combined with the grit and determination which had been instilled into me in the Army, I renewed my efforts and began training like a champion. I decided I would beat Douglas and settle the score.

Meanwhile, on the home front, Mary and I were having difficulties with our relationship. My immaturity was much to blame and although I may have deserved it, I was annihilated when Mary called it a day. She did it in such a normal and controlled manner that I couldn't believe what was happening. Looking back on it now I can see why our parents were against us getting engaged. We were too young and had our own insecurities and problems to sort out before entering into a mature and adult relationship. Love alone, and there was plenty of that, would not make things work for us.

I really lost it when we broke up. After that, any time I saw Mary at a club or disco, my heart would skip a beat. It took more than a year to get over her. She was such a decent girl but she couldn't cope with my paranoia and insecurities. Of course, the fact that she ended the relationship only served to increase my nightmare and I was on the edge of a nervous breakdown.

While this drama was unfolding, my younger brother Anthony was going out with a girl called Joanne Crowley, a very pretty girl, whom I was told had an older sister called Sharron. I was keen to see what she looked like and we met outside The Plough pub in Ilford. It was May 1985, three months before Sharron's seventeenth birthday. I thought she was really attractive and nice and we met up again at Bentley's nightclub in Canning Town. After that, we began dating almost immediately.

As with the other girls who had been special in my life,

my relationship with Sharron blossomed. For the first six months we could hardly let go of one another. We were so close and loving. Times were hard. I had no job and very little money and I was training as a fighter and had quit the flat which Mary and I shared. Even so, there was laughter in our lives.

Just five weeks after we met, Sharron told me she was pregnant. 'Great,' I said. 'Let's go for it.'

We were both so happy. I stayed with Sharron at her mum's house for a while and later we lived in a hostel while waiting for a council flat. In those days my ambitions were more down to earth. I thought if I could afford to buy us a terraced house, I would be fulfilled.

More people had begun to take notice of me as an amateur and my training was going well. I was putting in a lot of effort to face up to Rod Douglas and this time there would be no doubt about the outcome. Brian Lynch had taken over as my trainer and I thought he was the bee's knees. He was a jeweller who had been a Thames boatman and PE teacher and his approach to training was unorthodox, which attracted me to him in the first place.

My chance to even the score with Douglas came nearly a year after our first fight. We met for the ABA London division, part of the ABA national championship in 1986. This time it was a barn burner. Everyone came to watch. York Hall in Bethnal Green, where the fight was staged, was packed. Nobody who was on the amateur boxing circuit wanted to miss this fight. Around this time, I had told my brother John that the direction I wanted to take was now quite clear. I had regained my confidence and set my eyes on a fresh target. I would become the ABA champion and, from there, turn professional and become world champion.

John was amazed at how much I had progressed through the amateur ranks. In spite of that, he still thought my ambitious predictions were a little too optimistic. Even so, he was impressed by the enormous increase in my strength and power. As I progressed up the scale, boxing commentators who were conversant with top professional fighters around the world, began commenting on my power, speed and accuracy. They said it was as impressive as anything they had seen from Muhammad Ali, Sugar Ray Leonard, Marvin Hagler and George Foreman. When you're coming up the ranks, that's what you want to hear!

My mental attitude had also changed. I had set my sights on turning professional as soon as I had won the ABA nationals. I saw no future in getting hit for nothing. It would be madness to continue putting your body at risk for the sake of a hobby. Why get your head punched in for a trophy?

Brian Lynch trained me for the Douglas fight and put me through a hard routine, just like I had been used to in the Army.

I've said in the past that if you have a talent, exploit it to the full, and I was well aware that God had blessed me with the ability to fight. Steve Davis, the snooker player, was born to pot balls, Maradona to score goals and Nigel Benn to kick ass.

When I stepped into the ring with Douglas I instinctively knew I would beat him. I was as nervous as hell — after all, here I was fighting the same person in the same place where he had defeated me last time. But nervous adrenalin helped and it fed on the fact that the place was packed out. I'd put a lot in to win this fight and I was more hungry and more determined than before. Apart from that, I had done some growing up. We eye-balled each other and this time I had the eye of the tiger.

The last time we had been in the ring together, his greater experience in amateur boxing was a decisive factor. Not this time. I exploded, *Boom! Boom! Boom!* I had him down in the first round and again in the second or third. By the end of the fight I had clearly beaten him on points, in spite of the fact that he had been favourite. I then went on to beat Johnny Melfah in a further elimination round before going on to win the 1986 ABA national boxing championship cup.

My victory win put me in line to represent Britain in the Commonwealth Games in Edinburgh the same year but I was kicked out of the England squad by the ABA for allegedly missing the first training session. It seems the ABA favoured Rod Douglas in spite of my win and he was chosen to box for Britain and won the gold medal. I will never forgive the ABA for what it did to me. I felt cheated and humiliated by their decision. That gold should have been mine

Since becoming world champion, the ABA asked me to participate in various events and activities but I always refused. I won't help them now or in the future. The ABA acted like a judge and jury in a tragic case which had not come to court and in which they had no jurisdiction. They prejudged a personal issue when they had no right to do so and I shall hold that against them for as long as I live.

Sharron had given birth to our first child, Dominic, on 3 March 1986. The games were to be held in July. We were still living in one cramped room in a hostel with our young baby. We were young and inexperienced parents, having to survive in difficult conditions. In spite of this, we made the best of things and we both loved Dominic. We now have three children and our love for them has been the greatest thing in our lives.

After beating Douglas and winning the ABA national championships, I turned professional. Douglas stayed amateur and became the ABA title holder for the fourth time, while I went on to a win a series of fights which attracted the attention of the press and public. When he saw how successful I was as a professional boxer, Rod thought he'd follow suit and turned professional under Mickey Duff. He was hoping to fight me again, this time as a professional, before his career tragically ended on 25 October 1989 after 14 undefeated fights. The referee had to stop his British middleweight title contest against Herol Graham at Wembley in the ninth round after he'd been twice battered to the canvas. Rod went home feeling OK after the fight but collapsed three hours later and was lucky his brother drove him to hospital in time for neurosurgeons to remove a blood clot from his brain. It was his twenty-fifth birthday and he spent it first on the operating table and then on a life-support machine in intensive care.

That is one of the risks in boxing. In fact, his experience was very similar to the tragic events surrounding Michael Watson. Rod had to learn how to talk and walk all over again.

As a boxer, I have never allowed the thought of injury to interfere with my career. If I felt that way I wouldn't go on fighting. Tragically, I've seen it happen to people I like. I am very friendly with Michael Watson and although they tried to write him off, he is still a man, still a person. He has his wits about him, he knows what is going on, it's just that he hasn't recovered enough yet to be able to express it as effectively as he would like.

If you are going to be a successful fighter, you've got to turn away from the danger of physical hurt and protect yourself as best as you can while you fight. And once you're past it, you've got to know when to quit. I never wanted to be one of those fighters who keeps getting into the ring after his sell-by date. That's when you really *can* get hurt.

I have always tried to be level-headed about boxing. It's a question of sorting out your priorities, finding the right direction and attacking your target. As I keep saying, my army training really paid off. But long ago, when I had just started my professional career, I had already plotted my path. I said at the time that Britain had three world middleweight champions over the past 30 years. They were Randolph Turpin, Terry Downes and Alan Minter. Turpin was fighting before I was born and, having watched films of him in action, I rate him the best of the three. He could punch and he was a good boxer. Downes came second on my list because of his guts and courage and Alan Minter was third. My ambition was to top all three of them.

Brian Lynch had seen the potential in me as an amateur and I continued training with him for my professional fights, although we eventually parted company. Unfortunately, anybody who seems to have been involved with me always wants to take full credit for my fight victories. Brian and I were very close at first but, like others, he thinks, perhaps understandably, he taught me everything, how to punch and how to fight. That is a mistake which nobody should make. I taught myself how to fight. Others helped in sharpening up my skills. No trainer 'made' Nigel Benn.

If anyone made me it was Mum and Dad. If trainers or managers were that good, then why haven't they 'made' more Nigel Benns? That's the question they should be addressing. Furthermore, I twice became world champion *after* I left Brian. I learned a lot about controlling my aggression and channelling my strength in the Army. It was the Army that taught me the principle that force without judgement crashes by its own weight.

Having said that, I would not take away from the fact that Brian was a solid and good trainer. When I first began training with him, the ABA would not give him a coaching badge and West Ham club also turned him down so I trained in secret. Because of that, Brian had to function as my corner man in the crowd and he devised special signals which he would relay to me like a tick-tack man on a racecourse.

After I turned professional, however, he took out a trainer's licence and hired his own gym. We restricted sparring because there was little point in getting battered before a fight, and we also got rid of the old-style punch bag which used to injure quite a few fighters, even breaking their hands. For punching exercises, we used a floor-to-ceiling speedball and a swinging, lightweight sandbag. I would also shadow-box holding a 15lb barbell in each hand and run five to six miles a day, as well as play squash and do vigorous body-stretching exercises.

Brian was, in my opinion, a little too exacting in the beginning. Sometimes I thought he was hurting me excessively. He used to work me hard but, apart from some misgivings, I still think he was a good trainer, and I had been used to a tough routine in the Army. Difficult though it was, his training was right up my street. I knew I was in good shape and he would try to stretch me as far as he could. He was a big part of my life in those early professional days. He tried to be a father figure and, at the time, I thought that everything he was doing was for my benefit.

However, a certain amount of disillusionment set in. He put his son Sean in my corner at fights to 'keep it in the family', but how could a 17-year-old boy be in my corner? Only mature men should have been there. My dad thought it was wrong but didn't say anything. Afterwards, I thought that my brother John should have been my corner man. If we were going to keep it in the family, I would rather it was *my* family. After all, John had been a boxer. He was the one who introduced me to boxing and had encouraged me all along.

However, at the time I didn't want to upset Brian because we were so close. He would invite me to his lovely big house in Upminster and we would go to boxing matches together. One of the problems with him was that he thought he was right about everything. He had a jewellery shop in Hatton Garden, London, and another shop in Upminster and thought he was quite a powerful man and, like many successful men, that his influence could be applied to anything he was involved in. That didn't take into account the fact that I, too, had a strong personality and ideas of my own.

He used to train me three times a day but there is only so much a body will take. When I left him, I cut down my training to twice a day. He was working me to the bone and I found I couldn't take it any more. My body would say, 'Don't you think you are taking this too far?' I wanted to listen to my instincts but Brian kept impressing on me the need for hard training. I now think that is not proven. I've proved through my own success that you don't need to push things so far, that you should listen to what your body tells you and call it a day when you've had enough. No matter what any trainer might tell you, you can't argue the case against solid facts and results. My argument is backed up by two world titles.

7

THE BIGGER THEY COME ...

Burt McCarthy was stinking rich. He was a multi-millionaire and cousin of former British Featherweight Champion Sammy McCarthy. Burt had a nose for talented prospects and could smell success where this Ilford boy was concerned. A lot of people were beating a path in my direction after the ABA victory. Burt got there first and became my manager. News of my fighting style spread rapidly — Nigel Benn had come to town. Or, to be more accurate, the boxing fraternity had at last recognised him and were bringing out their welcome mats. I was about to throw away my learner plates and cross over into the fast lane from where I would never look back. What a metamorphosis it was!

I'd already seen some trappings of wealth with Brian Lynch but now Burt was displaying his like a peacock showing off his feathers: the flash mansion in Danbury, Essex, a penthouse in the Barbican and limousines which would need a wide-angle lens to fit them in the picture. Forget the fact that his money had not come from boxing but from other businesses. That didn't matter. It smelled good and I was hungry. 'You carry on doing the business,' he told me, 'and you'll get everything.'

Burt was a straight shooter and I respected his advice.

He inspired me to pursue the material gains which were there for the taking in professional boxing, providing, of course, that you were tops. He arranged my first fight against Graeme Ahmed on 28 January 1987 at Croydon, for which I was promised a purse of £1,000. That was a fortune to me then.

My professional début was on a Wednesday evening. Man, that's a night I won't forget. I weighed in at 11st 7¾lb, Ahmed at 11st 6½lb. I was raring to go, straining at the leash. But I was nervous, man, really, really nervous — before this fight I was even training in my sleep.

I got out there and the crowd was going wild, with me just thinking, 'I'm going to bash you, mate, I'm going to put you down.' I went for him in the first round, hitting him with some heavy-duty punches, but he stayed in close, and I couldn't quite nail him. I knew I had him in the second, though. As soon as the bell went, I put him down with a big left hook. He got up at nine, but went down twice more before the ref ended it.

I couldn't believe it was so easy, like counting 1-2-3. Respect to Ahmed, but it was a demolition job, and I felt great — £1,000 in my pocket, and he hadn't done me any damage. It was my first pro fight and it had gone the same way as all my army fights. But it was also my first lesson in professional fighting, which was a completely different kettle of fish to amateur boxing. I'd become a lot calmer and more focused in my training, so, after a couple of days off for some serious partying with Sharron (£1,000 could buy you a good time, and in those days the money always went as fast as I could earn it), I was back slogging away, training for my second match against Kevin Roper at Basildon, which was scheduled for 4 March.

The Welshman was heavier than me but the referee stopped the fight after 40 seconds in the first round. I was really cheesed off that night because they had almost started taking down the ring when it was our turn to fight. We'd got there at about 8.00pm and it wasn't until after midnight that we fought. The crowds didn't know who I was yet and I just wanted to get it over and done with. I gave Roper a right uppercut to his face and he retreated into a corner clutching his left eye. He was hurt badly and referee Davis called it off.

My next fight was against Bob Nieuwenhuizen of the Netherlands at the Albert Hall. I think he was the tallest guy I ever fought. He was about 6ft 5in. I needed a step-ladder to smack him in the mouth, he was so big. I thought someone was taking the mickey pitching us together. Why hadn't they brought in someone who was only 5ft 2in? I threw a left hook and hit him. I assaulted his body, *Boom, Boom, Boom!* I was really rushing about in the first few fights. I was always in first gear, never had time to get into second. Eventually, Nieuwenhuizen threw a jab at me and I returned with a left hook and thought, good night, hello Las Vegas! The referee rang the bell. The bigger they are, the harder they fall. The ref, Nick White, had stopped the fight after two minutes three seconds, even though the Dutchman beat the count and got up at eight.

Fight number four on Saturday, 9 May was against a good old pro, Winston Burnett, who was from Cardiff. This Welshman was a good campaigner and I reckon he wanted to survive to one hundred. However, I figured I'd put an end to that and, while he gave a good defence, I got him 45 seconds into the fourth round. I didn't think he came to fight. It seemed more like he was there to survive. He took a lot of punishment without reply but when he tried to smother me I landed a blow to the side of his head followed by a lot of punches to his body. I kept at him hammer and tongs in the fourth when referee Nathan stopped the fight.

The next month I fought American Reginald Marks at

the Albert Hall, Kensington, and he was out in the first round. I remember him clearly. He wore blue shorts and he was smaller than me. I just gave it to him. I knocked him about like he was a dead body. I had him on the ropes and was whacking him in the body before sending him down with a right to the top of his head. He jumped up and *bang!* I walloped him again with a left hook. Although he got up at about nine, referee Sower reckoned he'd had enough and called time after two minutes ten seconds.

I was back at the Albert Hall two weeks later on 1 July, fighting another American, Leon Morris, who, like Marks, was from Louisiana. He was a big guy who charged at me like a wounded buffalo. He punched me in the back of the head and on the side and then caught me behind the ear. I threw a left at him, which was more devastating, followed it through with another left hook and he went down like a lead weight. Somehow he wobbled up again after the count but couldn't stay there. He was like a baby learning to walk. They had to carry him out and he didn't know what time of day it was. The fight lasted 25 seconds of the scheduled eight rounds.

Eddie Smith had a good record and was a force to be reckoned with. He'd beaten Tony Sibson, Frank Wissenbach and Roy Gumbs in the past but went down to me after 68 seconds. A Manchester veteran, Eddie connected two left hooks to my head but I retaliated with a right uppercut and a damaging left hook followed by a series of left hooks. It was my seventh straight stoppage win and the fifth in one round.

Next, I stopped Winston Burnett for a second time in the third of six two-minute rounds at the Albert Hall on 16 September. Just before the bell went in the second, I hurt Burnett with a big right uppercut and then hammered him on the ropes. The ref, Sid Nathan, stopped the bout.

I'll never forget the punch I gave Russell Barker, a

Scotsman from Nottingham. People thought I'd killed him. He was a same-day substitute for Frank Warren's Seconds Out series.

Fight after fight, victory after victory, the money began rolling in and mounting up. People began to recognise me in the street, the boxing groupies couldn't get to the powder room fast enough. Did someone say fight groupies liked boxers because they were thick and strong?

When I started out, my ambitions were to own a terraced house and a BMW. Within months of turning pro, I had more offers of cars than I knew what to do with. Car dealers would sponsor me with BMWs, others would lend me their flashiest motors. One dealer had my name in huge letters down the side of the car. I was more conspicuous than a double-decker bus and didn't like that at all. It was uncanny being able to drive any car I wanted. I'd only recently got a driving licence and my only advanced training, necessary for some of the high-powered vehicles offered, was crashing into a lamp-post at Ford's.

I became a celebrity overnight. Only 18 months previously, I'd been on the dole and catching buses everywhere — providing I could afford them, which was not always the case. Stardom was bound to go to my head and it did, at least until I became accustomed to it. Amateur boxing had given me prizes but no cash. The only money I had received was from the social security office: about £38 a week, with which I had to support Sharron and Dominic while living in a hostel that gave us no privacy.

Our daughter Sadé (we pronounce her name Shaaday) was born the following year on 14 October 1987. She was the first girl in the family. All my brothers had produced boys up to that point and I was over the moon. My parents had always wanted a girl and now I had come up with the goods. I gave Mum what she had always wanted. Sadé was a cheerful, smiling, lovely little girl. I was overawed. But what a handful! She's DC — different class. Someone suggested to me recently that she might give me trouble when she grows up. I responded, 'No, she'll give someone else trouble. A young man will come to me one day and say, "Mr Benn, your daughter's breaking my ass." I'll say, "Hell, what do you think I had from the mother, then? All right? So leave it now and stop knocking on my door, or I'll set my Rottweiler on you. Piss off and leave me alone."'

Burt McCarthy was a good, clean, honest man who never took money off me until I got going. Sometimes I felt he pampered me too much. I wanted to get out there and fight and I mean *fight*, go at it hammer and tongs. But he gave me dead bodies to knock out. After a while, Burt wasn't sure that he could give 100 per cent to me. 'That could be unfair to a talent such as his. I might regret the decision a thousand times, but I can't do things by half. I feel it's better to leave him to somebody else,' he said. It was 1987, and after about 12 fights, I changed managers and went for one who had a lot more clout — Frank Warren.

Frank was confident about my prospects. He told the world that I could become a millionaire within the next three years and insisted I could take over from Frank Bruno as the biggest draw in British boxing. How right he was!

At the start, Frank Warren got me the fights I wanted. You get to a stage where you can't find mugs any more and you have to fight top guys. Frank told me, 'You want a title fight? I'll get you one.' And he did. Before we fell out, Frank was very kind to me. He lent me £10,000 as a deposit on my first house which I bought with Sharron in East Ham in 1988.

Ronnie Yeo became my next victim at Bethnal Green

on 3 November. He was from Tennessee and a very experienced boxer. He actually threw a punch at me and, before it could connect, mine had already struck him like an Exocet. It was a single punch knock-out and the referee didn't even bother taking up a count. Yeo crashed to the canvas in 57 seconds of the first round. He was really hurt.

Ian Chantler was a southpaw (left-handed) who helped create the record for my fastest fight. I laid him out in 16 seconds. He was like a new-born foal trying to get up and not quite making it. While he was on the floor, he made swimming and flying motions like a clumsy swan. That was my quickest KO ever. All he had time to do was walk to the centre of the ring and try three jabs — none of which connected.

My twelfth and final fight in my first year as a professional was a milestone in every sense of the word. It was against Reggie Miller at the Albert Hall on 2 December and I KO'd him in the seventh, but he made me work for it. This was the longest I'd ever fought. Up until this time, my fights had never gone beyond the fourth round. I thought that if he could stay on his feet he might even snatch victory so I had to pull it out of the bag. He made me realise there was another level which I had not yet reached. The Dark Destroyer wasn't doing his job fast enough on this one and Miller was the only person who ever made me feel that I had to change.

I wasn't expecting such a hard fight but I was, nevertheless, confident that I would win. He was taller than me, and two pounds heavier, and he had me on the ropes a few times. The only time I got him, I went *boom* with my left and it exploded on his chin. He went down and his legs caved in. It was a good fight and I was pleased for the competition. I should have been fighting American Kenny 'The Blizzard' Snow who had won 28 of his 30 fights but he had to cancel. After the fight I felt proud of myself because I had wanted to prove I wasn't a one-minute wonder knocking over bums and I did that. Miller was a somebody, his record showed that and he caught me with some good hooks. I had showed the critics that I could take a good punch as well as give one.

By this time I was itching for a title fight, impatient for a place on the world ratings list which only my idols, Mike Tyson, who was number one heavyweight and WBC, WBA and IBF champion, and Marvin Hagler, number one middleweight, appeared. The middleweight list gave me most of my targets. At that time, the 15 top fighters were Marvin Hagler (USA), Thomas Hearns (USA), Sumbu Kalambay (Italy), Frank Tate (USA), Mike Nunn (USA), Mike McCallum (Jamaica), Michael Olajide (Canada), Herol Graham (England), Chong Pal Park (Korea), Lindell Holmes (USA), Robbie Sims (USA), Donald Lee (USA), Tony Sibson (England) and Roberto Duran (Panama). I wanted to see the name Nigel Benn in the number one slot.

My career was to change dramatically after a chance meeting with Ambrose Mendy at a club in the West End. It was on the night I had been lent a Bentley by Richard Clements, a car dealer, and pretended to everyone that I owned it. I was only 24, and went with three mates to various clubs up West, giving it *large*. Extra large, in fact. When I drove the car, people showed a lot of respect and courtesy. I thought it was me at first, but then I realised it was the car they were admiring. I suppose that's when my love of flash cars started.

Ambrose and I started chatting and he was giving me all these big words. I was impressed. He was DC — he looked good, dressed expensively, talked big. I thought he was the business. He was the first black man I had seen who I thought had it all. I'd never met anyone like him before. I thought he was the best thing since sliced bread. Afterwards, he invited me to his large home in Wanstead.

This was real money. A swimming pool in the back
garden and two Mercedes parked in the drive. Here was a
man who had done very well for himself. He was giving
me a lot of patter — so much that I thought this is the man
for me.

8

MENDY v WARREN

F rank Warren and Ambrose Mendy both had important roles in my fight career. I have got on fine with Frank Warren since he and American impresario Don King staged my later fights. He's a good promoter and has become a much calmer person following his shooting in the East End of London.

However, when he was my manager in the first half of 1988, disillusionment set in because I wanted his individual attention. At the same time, I was becoming more susceptible to the silver-tongued eloquence of Ambrose Mendy. Fate decreed that our fortunes would be closely linked.

Ambrose became involved in my affairs as he did with several other sporting personalities, including Terry Marsh, a mutual friend. Terry had also been managed by Frank Warren and had stayed with me in Miami prior to his arrest for the attempted murder of Frank. He was acquitted at the Old Bailey.

All of us — Frank, Ambrose and I — each had strong wills of our own. With that combination, life was never guaranteed to run smoothly. Frank was from Islington, north London. His dad was a bookie and the family branched out into entertainment. They sold juke boxes, pinball tables and cigarette machines to pubs.

Frank had left school at 15 and had been a salesman and meat porter before becoming involved in the leisure business. While I had once fought as a prize fighter, through his contacts in pubs Frank began staging fights. They were unlicensed by the British Boxing Board of Control, but licensed by the NBCL, and promoting them fired his entrepreneurial spirit. Eventually, it led to his manager's licence, after a battle with the boxing establishment. Most of the London venues and boxers were dealt with by Mickey Duff, Terry Lawless, Jarvis Astaire and Harry Levine but Frank broke in.

He then got a promoter's licence and was on his way to becoming one of the most powerful men in boxing in the UK.

Frank is a man who likes nothing better than making deals. Occasionally, we would socialise in clubs. Frank had quite a lot of style. However, Frank's worst moment came on a cold November evening in 1989 when he stepped out of his chauffeur-driven Bentley which had brought him to a boxing match in Barking. He was shot with a 9mm bullet fired from an automatic Luger pistol, which nearly cost him his life. The bullet missed his heart by an inch, and the others that followed took away part of his lung. To top it all, surgeons then discovered that they would also have to remove a benign thyroid tumour. He lost a lot of weight in hospital which he put down to 'lead plan diet'. He always had a good sense of humour. Mickey Duff later quipped that Frank had learned many lessons in life: 'One of them is to duck.'

I always admire people who get up and go and Frank did just that. After the shooting his business empire was in trouble. But Frank is back today and has joined forces with Don King who is probably the richest fight promoter in the world, worth about £500 million.

Ambrose was Mr Charm. He was full of charisma and hype and had everyone intrigued with stories about himself. Apart from running his company, World Sports Corporation, from plush offices near Tower Bridge, he was also trade development counsellor for the West African state of Guinea-Bissau. He once told a court his business was 'hype'. He said, 'If we are promoting an event, we are responsible for the hype. We are in the business of PR and creating press relations and secreting information to the press, especially the tabloid press. So that if you see a world exclusive, we would have been responsible for passing the information to the journalists. We have to develop as much hype as possible so that there is a clamour for tickets. Hype moves at a pace. Yesterday's *news is yesterday's blues.'*

From growing up in Hackney and running a stall in Islington selling children's clothes (that's where he met Frank Warren), Ambrose was now involved with some really big sporting personalities. They included my cousin Paul Ince, John Fashanu, Linford Christie, Ellery Hanley and Terry Marsh. He always has interesting observations to make. 'Charisma is a way, not a play. You can't rent charisma by the day.'

While other people might shoot from the hip, Ambrose shot from the mouth. He would fire off about anything and make it seem funny. He told one interviewer, 'It's a dog-eat-dog, bullshit society. So you've got to take as much as you can for as little as you can fairly give. Fairly is the operative word. I don't have a contract with anyone I represent. It's all done on a handshake. If they want to walk away, they walk.'

Ambrose was an educated man. He was the fourth of eleven children and left school with three A-levels. His further education was in prison. At the age of 22 he was sent inside for six years. In four years he was moved around 21 prisons but made good use of his time studying finance and marketing. I was totally impressed with the quotes and sayings he would come out with.

With these two people in the background, I continued my run of successes in the ring. My first fight in 1988 was against Fermin Chirinos at Bethnal Green on 27 January. He was from Venezuela and a good old warhorse. I sparked him in two.

Just ten days later, I had to fight Canadian Byron Prince at Stafford on 7 February. It was at Tony Sibson's challenge for Frank Tate's IBF title at Bingley Hall. Although I won my bout, I didn't see the title fight because CS gas was squirted in my and Sean Lynch's face as we were walking back to the ring after my victory.

John, my brother, was there as well but he didn't get hurt. One side of Sean's face was burnt and I began vomiting and was rushed to hospital. Police thought the problems involved Sibson supporters in Leicester and my supporters in London but John said the Leicester crowd were trying to get revenge on London lads whom they wrongly thought had been our supporters. He said stewards had to separate the warring factions and that the Leicester mob had got a kicking after Tony Sibson beat Mark Kaylor in London.

Prince was big and tough, but there was no way the Dark Destroyer was going to be scared of him. I never had any fear of my opponents. I was nervous but never afraid. I don't think fear is an emotion I will ever feel again after serving in Northern Ireland. When I got out there, it seemed more like he was slapping me than punching me before I KO'd him on his feet.

Nearly three weeks later, on 24 February, I fought Greg Taylor at Aberfan in Wales. He was an American who really fancied himself. I split both of his eyelids and blood was gushing out. He was bashed from pillar to post. I still remember him exclaiming, 'Goddamn!' when the referee stopped the fight after one minute in the second round. Even though blood was flowing from his nose and eyes, he didn't want to stop. He was bad-mouthing me and needling me before the start, trying to wind me up. That got me in the right frame of mind, especially when he kept saying, 'You're gonna go.' I was determined to make him pay.

On 14 March I had another easy victory at Norwich, fighting Darren Hobson from Leeds. He was a good, average fighter who thought he was the next Nigel Benn. Do me a favour! He brought his amateur style into professional ranks and was out in the first round — history. I wanted a real fight. 'Come on, Frank,' I said, 'give me a fight!'

I didn't have long to wait. Warren arranged for me to fight Ghanian Abdul Umaru Sanda for the vacant Commonwealth middleweight title at Muswell Hill on 20 April. I thought I would have to work hard here. Sanda was big, tall and gangly but I had good support down there.

'Go for your dreams,' I thought to myself. I felt confident and did a lot of bobbing and swaying to make him miss me. He had lots of experience and I thought I would just have to cut him down. I was bashing his body and giving it to him left and right. I was having a field day. The ref was telling me to calm down. I bashed Sanda over in the first round and did him in the second. I went steaming in.

The ref was pulling me back and, at one stage, had hold of both my arms behind my back. At the end of the fight, I dropped to my knees and shouted a victory cry. It was my moment of glory although, afterwards, I was criticised by Les McCarthy, Burt's brother, who objected to my antics. I resented his intrusion. He wouldn't have got in the ring and fought like I did. I deserved that.

Muhammad Ali went berserk when he beat Liston and

Sugar Ray Leonard did exactly as I did after he beat Marvin Hagler. I'd just hammered a fighter who had never been stopped and won my first title. Nobody's going to tell me I can't celebrate a little.

My fight against American loud-mouth Tim Williams was to be my last with Frank Warren as my manager. It was arranged for 28 May at the Albert Hall. Williams, who had drawn with Marvin Hagler's half-brother Robbie Sims, looked like an elf. He was ugly as sin but with a good body and physique. He was mouthing me off like nothing on earth but then I always welcomed that because I could go ahead and kick ass badly. He had a good reputation in America and was rated as the 27th best middleweight in the world.

It took him four minutes to go down.

My reputation had reached new heights by this time. I was on a high, and everyone was predicting that I was seriously going places in the world of professional boxing. I'd won my first title, I was unbeaten, and I was getting nearer to my goal of being a world champion.

Flushed with victory, I had to make a decision whether to stay with Frank or go with Ambrose. As far as Frank was concerned, I felt I had more than given myself to his cause. Frank had arranged for me to fight American Eddie Hall at Luton Town Football Club on 25 June on the same bill as Barry McGuigan. I walked out on him 48 hours before I was due to appear. I had a different battle on my hands now.

9

SVENGALI

My boxing career really took off with Ambrose Mendy. At the time, he was the best thing for me. Ambrose was more than my mentor. He took the place of Andy, the older brother I loved and missed so much. He was charismatic and intelligent. He was my very own Milk Tray man with all the mystery, intrigue and looks of James Bond 007.

I loved him more than any other person. At the time, he was as important to me as Sharron. That is why, when it all went sour a few years later, I was deeply hurt and would never have another manager. When Sharron and I married, he was my best man. I modelled myself so much on Ambrose. He looked good. He was an attractive, well-manicured man about ten years older than me, who looked as if he'd never done a day's work in his life and had loads of front. From the way he spoke, you would have thought he had a posh education but I know he'd improved himself in prison.

Although he came from the street, he had the charm and class of a gentleman. But he did it without looking tacky and I learned a lot from him. Ambrose conducted business with flair. Admittedly he would sometimes be on another planet or in cloud cuckoo land but then he was also the sort of person who could make you believe that day was night.

He was the Don King of Britain. He had everything and I ended up loving him like a brother. Dad was not so ready to accept him, though. He warned me off him and told me not to trust Mendy. He was right, but I only found that out much later.

Ambrose liked doing things in style. He gave me lots of incentive and ideas. We did everything together and I tried to emulate his lifestyle. 'If you've got it, flaunt it' was the message. At his persuasion, I bought a Porsche on hire purchase. It cost me £4,000 a month! He made me live big but that never did me any harm. It helped me to think in telephone numbers when negotiating the purse for a fight. He showed me where I was going and I always thought that if I had a problem, Ambrose would be there to sort it out. And he was. He could be relied on to be there for me whenever I needed him.

We'd go down nearly every day to his office at Tower Bridge. It was a sumptuous loft conversion in black and pine and he'd lean back in his leather chair with the air of somebody very important. Ambrose had about three or four employees: Natalia, Georgiana, Tony and Jackie. Natalia thought the sun shone from his backside. She, like him, had more bullshit than anybody I had ever come across. She tried to emulate Ambrose and also covered up for him. Like them, I thought he was God.

It was only later that I asked myself: 'How come Ambrose is the one with two Mercedes and a large house in Wanstead with a swimming pool and gardeners, when I'm the one taking the punches and all I've got is a three-bedroom terrace?'

Ambrose would make me laugh at the things he came out with and his bare-faced cheek was incredible. He would tell a bank manager of 20 years' standing how to do his job. It seemed like he knew everything about business and I was impressed then, and still am now, with his flair. His wife Jennifer, however, was not my cup of tea. I felt she was less down-to-earth than I was. I had no pretensions but Ambrose would believe his own hype. He got me a lot of press coverage. At the same time, however, he was building his own platform.

Frank Warren was furious that Ambrose had become involved with me. He warned me, 'Walk out on me and you won't find it so easy to get good fights.' There was no love lost between us in those days. Frank was particularly angry that I had pulled out of the open-air show at Luton in June 1988 where Barry McGuigan topped the bill.

My fight with Eddie Hall was to be the chief support bout and a lot of people had bought tickets to see me. Warren's plans for me to fight in Las Vegas the following month, as chief support for the world middleweight fight between Frank Tate and Michael Nunn, had also fallen through and, once again, I wanted more attention.

I was seriously considering quitting Britain for America at this time because I was attracting a lot of flak from all quarters. It seemed that, having achieved some success, people were now jealous of that and were gunning for me. Britain appeared much more comfortable with failures like Eddie the Eagle than with successes like Nigel Benn.

My former manager, Burt McCarthy, from whom Warren had taken over, said my career could be ruined by my walk-out.

Frank, no stranger to courts, immediately issued writs and said I was being misled by my advisers. He said, 'The people who are telling him what to do are a joke. Nigel is being advised by a bunch of half-wits and I will be serving writs on everyone involved. He has broken his contract by not going through with this fight. I know he's had a lot of publicity but he must keep his feet on the ground. He's missed a golden opportunity in front of American television. He can't sign contracts and then walk out on them just because he feels like it. I'm not going to let him renege on a contract. It's a matter of principle and I'm not going to give in over this.'

Frank insisted that our contract had more than two years seven months to run, with a further three-year option, and vowed he would enforce it. He won a High Court battle stopping me from signing a contract with Mendy pending further legal action.

In the meantime, however, I had also sued Frank. My writ disputed the validity of his management agreement. I then went back to court and won the battle to discharge the injunction ordering Mendy not to interfere in the contractual relationship between Warren and me.

Another weapon Frank tried to use at the time was the British Boxing Board of Control (BBBC), for whom I did not have any time then or now. They would not license Mendy and I was even threatened with losing my licence and being stripped of my Commonwealth championship if I had dealings with him. Later, Ambrose devised a plan of revenge which I carried out. I tore up my British boxing licence on television.

I also let it be known at the time that I no longer wanted to fight cadavers in the ring. I wanted real fighters like Herol Graham, Michael Watson and Johnny Melfah. While this was going on, Barry Hearn held talks with me about the prospect of teaming up.

I was angry over the whole affair. It was getting nasty and got very close to a punch-up between me and Frank. He didn't *own* me. Nobody owns me. At one point, I felt like going round and working him over and I guess he felt the same about me.

Because of the bust-up, I did not fight for nearly five months. On 12 September 1988, Mr Justice Pill lifted the injunction stopping Mendy from acting for me. That left me free to box under my own management and I stepped into the ring with Anthony Logan at the Albert Hall on 26 October to defend my Commonwealth middleweight championship.

For some inexplicable reason, TV stations did not want to cover the event which was surprising considering how much they had plugged my earlier fights. We were assured that it had nothing to do with my TV walk-out from the Luton bout when I split with Frank. Promoter Mike Barrett who offered the rights was turned down flat. Mike's co-promoters for the fight were Terry Marsh and Frank Maloney.

Both the BBC and ITV denied it was a deliberate blackout but as it turns out, by not putting it on they deprived fans of an exciting match. I was convinced that Frank, Barry Hearn and Mickey Duff were able to call the shots over TV coverage, and they certainly weren't able to do much for me then.

Logan had had just over two years' professional experience and had scored 14 wins in 16 bouts. He lost to David Noel of Trinidad before our fight and, until then, held a number 18 rating from the WBC. It was also Logan's first defence of his Continental Americas title which he had won five months earlier when he beat Argentinian Ramon Abeldano in Trinidad. He was also a good puncher and had had five first-round wins between November 1987 and February of the next year.

As far as I was concerned, Logan was the ugliest, most horrible opponent I could wish for. He was a right mouthy fucker — he kept going on about how he was going to bash me up. I detested him. I thought he was a horrible, horrible person. I had no respect for him and just fought to get rid of this man. As part of his pre-match hype, he said the opponents I had beaten were garbage. If that was the case, I was determined to add his remains to the scrap heap.

The Royal Albert Hall was packed. Logan had wound me up something rotten and I was trying to knock him out to teach him a lesson. But he caught me, crash, bang, wallop on the chin and over I went. I was up by the count of one and he was catching me with a lot of punches. He hit me 22 times. A lot of people do that but then forget their own defence. I thought, if you hit me 22 times and can't knock me out, it must be ta-ta to you.

I threw a left and saw him screwing up his face. All of a sudden he was the one on the canvas, in spite of all those punches he'd thrown at me. Out, mate! His eyes were rolling in his head and his mouth was open like a stunned fish. That hit did it for him. He wobbled up and the crowd went whooping mad with delight. Many people had doubted me up until then and, even afterwards, were saying mine was a lucky punch but I was going for it. It wasn't lucky. When they go, they go!

Dad and Mum had always come to my fights. Dad wouldn't miss a single one, ever since I had partly blamed him for losing to Rod Douglas in our first amateur fight. I had told Dad that if he'd been there, I would have beaten Douglas both times. Dad told me, 'I didn't know how serious you were. If you want to go into boxing you need to go into it 100 per cent. Not 95. If you're really serious, I will be there for every fight.' And he was. They were all very proud of me and I was happy that my parents both came to watch. After Logan, however, we banned Mum from further bouts.

Dad tells the story better than me because he was right there next to Mum. He said, 'We were all keen to see this fight. It was like a comeback fight after Nigel's problems with Frank Warren. Mum had settled down expecting Nigel to do his normal thing — which was to hit the other person and not get hit much himself.

'Instead, he went down in the first round and Mum wasn't pleased. Not at all. She kept looking at him and turning to me. In the second round, Nigel took all those punches without throwing one back at first and Mum decided she'd had enough. "Stop the fight," she demanded. I told her to sit down. She wouldn't. She yelled out, "Stop that man hitting my son." We were at the ringside and there she was ordering me to get in the ring and break up the fight!

'Fortunately, Nigel did the business and knocked out Logan before she had a chance to finish the fight spectacularly herself. I then turned to her and said, "See, your son has just knocked out somebody else's son. What do you want me to do now?" I told her, "You're not coming back no more."'

It felt really good to put Logan down, but if I'm honest I can't say I was particularly proud of my performance. It turned into more of a street fight than a boxing match — two big guys brawling because they didn't like each other much. I completely flipped, and afterwards Brian Lynch, my trainer, told me, 'If you fight like that again, I'm finished with you.' Man, he was mad!

After the fight, Frank Warren wanted to make up with me and start afresh but there was no way I'd agree to it. Ambrose was firmly entrenched as my mentor. Warren said he only had my interests at heart and urged that he didn't want to see me go the way of John Conteh. He said of me: 'He is in danger of making the same mistakes that wrecked John Conteh's career. He is trying to go too fast, too soon ... he needs my help.' Frank went on to deny that, apart from one or two exceptions, he'd only got stiffs for me to fight and claimed I was fighting proper people and was being paid more money than any boxer at the same stage of my career.

Needless to say, his arguments failed to convince me

then, although there is no doubt that he is now the number-one man in boxing in Britain.

My next opponent was David Noel of Trinidad. We were scheduled to fight at Crystal Palace on 10 December. He'd beaten Logan on points over 12 rounds and boasted how he'd never been knocked down during his 20 fights. Of his 35 contests, he had lost only four. He was now challenging me for my Commonwealth middleweight crown. I thought it would be another humdinger of a fight, but he got bashed up good. Real good. I thought he'd last at least six rounds. He was out in one.

I was now one step closer to fighting Michael Watson and getting my biggest purse ever: £150,000. I had challenged Herol Graham to a bout but nothing came of it. Everything seemed at last to be going well for me. I was happy to have Ambrose and my purse had increased enormously and was now set to multiply many times more. My social life was also becoming more hectic. I had a lot of celebrating to do in the little time between fights and that was an important part of my life. I didn't want to blow my money like a lot of boxers do but then I didn't want to be the richest man in the graveyard either. I wanted to enjoy my money. I had a small circle of close mates and a large circle of hangers-on. When I was not training, it was party time.

10

THE ORGY

R olex Ray could talk his way into anywhere. He's blond, good looking and smooth as silk. He also happens to be rich. We met at the Berkeley Square ball and were introduced by Ambrose. I'd seen Ray around before then, however, because we liked the same music and clubs. Money was never an object with Ray. Like me, he was an Essex lad and since meeting, he's become one of my best mates. We shared a lot in common and found that we'd been to the same clubs in Ilford, such as Lacy Ladies, the Mocca and Dagenham Town Hall.

We called him Rolex Ray because he dealt in jewellery and specialised in genuine, second-hand, gold Rolex and Cartier watches at reasonable prices. I bought my diamond-studded gold Cartier from him.

With my busy fight schedule and training, Ray was a little concerned that I had been working too hard and not having enough fun so he organised an outing for us. 'I want to take you to a party, Nige,' he said. 'It's going to be very special.'

We drove from Ilford to a huge detached house in the Surrey stockbroker belt, arriving early in the evening. It was a warm summer's night. I didn't know what to expect because Ray was keeping that a surprise. We hardly found space to park with all the expensive motors parked haphazardly in the grounds and on the roadside adjoining the property — Bentleys, Rolls-Royces, Jaguars and Daimlers littered the driveway. Some had chauffeurs who had made themselves comfortable on the back seats with books and thermos flasks and were prepared for a long night's wait. Ray either knew somebody there or chatted up the doorman and we were whisked inside.

The sight that met my eyes was unbelievable. I had never ever seen anything like it before. A mass orgy had been staged with an invitation list that read like a page from *Who's Who*. There were bankers, doctors, actors, well-known personalities and members of the aristocracy. What they all seemed to have in common was wealth. Those women who still had their clothes on were beautifully and expensively dressed. One lady reminded me of the actress Lesley Ann Down, though she clearly wasn't — she was exquisite. Among show business personalities were top TV actors whose faces I had seen on some of the most popular series.

This was dream time for me. I was an ordinary lad from east London — Essex boy from Ilford meets high society in deepest Surrey. It might as well have been outer Mongolia as far as I was concerned. It was a total culture shock. So this was how the rich lived!

Ray had been to three or four orgies before so I looked to him for guidance. The owner of the house was in the porn movie business and 80 per cent of the guests were married couples. Everyone had to come as a couple, otherwise they would not be admitted. We were the exception. Ray had got us in on who I was. The house had six bedrooms and the host had locked every single window, bolted them and taken away the keys. All doors had been taken off their hinges on the top floor and, instead of beds, four-inch-thick foam covered the floors and became one giant mattress.

Despite the fact that it was midsummer, the central heating had been turned on full, making it unbearably hot to keep your clothes on. A lot of the women were outrageously dressed. Stockings, suspenders, chains attached to nipples, black Gestapo jack-boots and tiny maids' outfits. There was a dress to fulfil every fantasy and a willingness by partygoers to make the fantasy a reality.

No pressure was put on anybody to join in. You could be a voyeur or participant, whatever you wanted. Downstairs, there was a bar and DJ and disco which looked just like a normal party. But upstairs — that was something else.

Ray said, 'Come on, Nige, let's get in there.' That was his cue for stripping down to our G-strings and dancing in the disco. We were the first to strip off and then everybody joined in. Ray always takes the mick out of me when it comes to taking off my clothes. He says I can't wait to show myself off in my G-string and claims I'm a Chippendale at heart. That's not true. However, with all the training I do, my body is in good shape. We were the catalyst the group was waiting for. Everybody began following our example by dressing down, some to their G-strings, others went totally nude.

I really think I'm much better in a one-to-one relationship, or in a threesome, than with so many people. It was too much. There were so many beautiful women, hair immaculate, bedecked in jewels, entirely naked and begging you — or their husbands begging you on their wives' behalf — to make love to them. It blew my mind. I couldn't believe it was so open. I watched, a little shocked, as one girl made love with three men who catered to her every fantasy. She was astride one man, another was leaping doggy-fashion on to her, and a third was kneeling in front of her while she performed oral sex on him.

I was a bit put off when I saw a man making oral love

to a woman and a third party came with a bottle of champagne which he poured over her private parts saying, 'That's to improve the flavour.' Wives were making love to each other watched by their husbands. It was a total, total shock. It's not that I'm prudish but I was only about 24 and this was the first time I had seen it done in public. A couple of girls came to Ray and me and offered us oral sex and later the Lesley Ann Down lookalike asked me to make love to her.

'Not here,' I said. 'No way.'

Had she been willing to come to our stretch limousine, it might have been another matter but I wasn't going to perform in front of all those people. I didn't fancy 20 sets of eyes, moving like yo-yos, watching my bobbing backside in this public arena.

Some time during the evening, an old couple approached us. He was about 70 and his wife 60. Ray opened the lady's blouse and asked, 'What have you got in there, then?' I was giggling and laughing and telling him not to do it. But it must have turned her husband on because he took hold of his wife's hand and pushed it on to my nuts and asked her if she fancied a bit of black. I said, '*No chance!* I ain't doing that, and if that old bastard does that again I'll break her finger and flatten her husband's bald head!'

But it was all said with a laugh. In the meantime, I was followed around by another beautiful lady, watched in the background by her husband. I thought if my wife got up to this sort of thing, I would chin the guy and her as well.

One of Ray's mates, who'd come there with a couple of girls, then played a joke on his chauffeur. The girls were sent out to chat up the driver and sneak him into the orgy. The chauffeur had been told to stay well clear of the house but the temptation offered by two mini-skirted, bra-less beauties with breasts hanging out of skimpy tops and the air thick with promise was too much.

Led by the giggling seductresses, he was taken into the house by the back door and brought to a small downstairs room which had a guest bed. The girls undressed him in no time at all and then chained him naked to the bed. Then they left him there and, five minutes later, his boss walked in pretending he didn't know anything about it and gave him a right bollocking for daring to come inside. Everyone witnessing the poor guy's dilemma was in fits of laughter but the poor man was scared witless and totally helpless, unable even to cover up his nakedness which now embarrassed him.

Ray pointed out two famous TV actors to me: one from *Coronation Street*, and another who had been in the popular TV series *The Avengers*.

Ray was more used to these parties than me and had a good time with several ladies, one of them a publican's wife. Her husband had approached him and said, 'My wife really likes you,' so Ray, ever the gentleman, obliged. However, he was a bit aghast when the husband invited him to their pub for Sunday lunch. Ray told him that would be too early in the day

The publican replied, 'We have a football team. We all go and play football and then the whole team comes back to the pub and makes love to the missus. We do that every Sunday and you're invited to join the team!'

I got home at about 6.30 the next morning, went straight to Mum and Dad's and said, 'Guess where I've been.' I told them everything and they killed themselves laughing. I still hadn't got over the shock of it all. Having said that, I was no novice to sexual adventure, providing, as I said, it wasn't in front of an audience.

People tend to treat you differently if they think you are a celebrity. A lot of people thought that, as a boxer, I shouldn't have as much fun as I did because I should concentrate on training. Well, they can think again. I like the attention from time to time, but I've given up trying to convince people that I am no different to them. So-called celebrities have just the same problems with wives, partners and mates as everybody else. I like to think that once outside the boxing ring, I'm Joe Bloggs, ordinary citizen.

Just because I train a lot doesn't mean that I can't have fun while I'm working. That's a load of tosh. I spent my time mucking about and it didn't seem to do me any harm in my career. As far as I'm concerned, it's unhealthy to lock yourself away. Even when I was in the final six weeks of training for a fight and had stopped the partying, I still went out and had lots of fun. However, I was always mindful that there may be another young Nigel Benn lurking in the shadows ready to take over.

With the amount of press coverage I was getting, there were bound to be lots of ladies interested in meeting me, although I never had problems in that department before becoming a professional boxer. One of the nicest girls I met at the Ilford Palais was Mandy. She was tall and very thin with a lovely pair of breasts. I've always liked women dressing in sexy clothes and Mandy knew how to please. She wore tight fish-net stockings and a skimpy top.

The sexy garments sent out the right messages but Mandy wasn't going to be a push-over. I was about 24 and she was 18. I was dying to see what was underneath those alluring clothes but when, eventually, I persuaded her to return to a mate's apartment she refused to let me make love to her. I tried for five hours and when, at last, she relented, it was all over in a few seconds. The tension and wait had taken their toll.

We kept seeing each other for the next two years and she was one of the sexiest girls I knew. Once we got to know each other properly, she'd be happy to make love anywhere. I'm fairly nocturnal in my habits and sometimes it would be too late to visit my friends, so one night Mandy and I made love on the bonnet of my Porsche in a wrecker's yard at 5.00am!

The setting may not have been the most romantic but it was fun and exciting and sexy. We were always doing dares. Once we made love down an alleyway and also in the ladies' toilets at Jacqueline's, a West End club.

It was run by my agent, Dave Simones, who insists on stealing food off my plate or from my kitchen at home. Maybe he just gets a bit hungry but he won't buy his own food. Once I chased him with a knife and threatened to kill him if he opened my refrigerator door once more. Dave thought it was all a joke but I was deadly serious. When he was running the club, we'd have some really fun times, although there was always an element of danger with the beautiful girls who'd go there. Like the one on my stag night with whom I ended up in bed.

I don't know how that came about because I was out of it — drunk as a lord. On this particular evening, I could have rewritten the fairytale of the frog and the princess. The standard version goes like this. The princess kisses a frog which then turns into a prince and they live happily ever after. Well, I kissed a frog and she turned into a princess but the next day when I woke up and kissed her again she turned back into a frog. I was so drunk I didn't know what I was doing.

I found myself in bed with this girl and woke with a dazed head to find that she had been giving me oral sex. The night before she was Marilyn Monroe. Now when I looked at her I saw Miss Piggy. That would have been almost acceptable were it not for the fact that I was panicking because my wife was due to pick me up at the hotel!

On another occasion I met a really tall girl. She was over 6ft tall but lovely with it. She had a great body, sparkling blue eyes and the figure of a model. We were discussing fantasies and I asked her about hers.

'I'd like to fuck two men on a football pitch,' she said.

That rather shocked me, coming from lips which I thought wouldn't melt butter, let alone talk dirty. And two men! Women surprise me all the time. I told her that I could partially fulfil her fantasies.

'I can get another man, I said, 'but I'm sorry about the football pitch.'

With that, I telephoned Ray who came round and we shared the young lady's favours. She was particularly physical and whenever Ray was flagging a little, I had to encourage him by pressing his backside down a little more energetically than he was inclined.

After the love-making, though, it was back to serious training and my next fight. At 24, a body can put itself through a much heavier and demanding pace than at, say, 30.

Life was never dull when Ambrose was involved in my affairs. He and my promoter had another bust-up with television before my next Commonwealth middleweight title defence against Zambian Michael Chilambe. He was popularly known as the African Lion and was ranked 26th in the world.

However, it was said he would have to run like a cheetah to stay upright for more than two or three rounds with me. The BBC had offered a derisory sum to screen the bout and my promoter Frank Maloney rejected it out of hand. ITV later came up with a suitable offer.

Frank had gone to Africa to find an opponent after 15 top American and European middleweights refused the opportunity of fighting me. Chilambe was my third challenger and had fought more than 200 amateur bouts.

He'd won 13 of his 14 professional fights with seven KOs.

Our fight was scheduled for 8 February at the Albert Hall and there was a real danger I would miss it as a result of a photofit picture, uncannily similar to me, of a wanted gunman and mugger who had blasted a cyclist at close range with a shotgun in Battersea Park.

Apparently the victim, who had been shot in the thigh, had identified his attacker by pointing to my picture in a magazine. The *Evening Standard* then published a slightly touched up photograph they had received from Scotland Yard and the first I knew about it was when a member of the public jumped on me, attempting a citizen's arrest. In the scuffle, I bruised my knuckle which became quite swollen and I had to receive intensive treatment before I could fight.

In fact, the doctors used a special, vibrating black box normally used to heal injured race horses. I was desperate for the hand to heal because I was still impatient to fight Michael Watson, having got nowhere with our offers to Herol Graham who was the current British Champion. We'd offered him £200,000 to put his British title on the line against me. After they'd heard about my injuries and Ambrose's threatened action regarding the photofit picture, both Scotland Yard and the newspaper apologised profusely for their mistake.

On top of everything else, I nearly had a bust-up at the press conference publicising the title defence. Anthony Logan, who was boxing on the undercard and had been sparring with Chilambe, was asked his opinion on how the bout would go. Instead of commenting on that, he asked for a return round with me. I'd beaten him the previous October and, as far as I was concerned, he was history. I was stopped from getting closer to him at the conference because somebody feared I might land one on him. They claimed they heard me say, 'I'm going to hurt you,' but I don't recall that.

The African Lion turned out to be a cub. I gave him a mauling and he went down in just 67 seconds of the first round. It should have been sooner, but I wanted to see if he could give anything worthwhile.

Chilambe said afterwards that he had never been hit so hard before. He said he knew I was a big hitter but hadn't realised just how big.

My next victory was in the High Court seven days later, when three Appeal Court judges dismissed Frank Warren's attempt to obtain a temporary order stopping Ambrose from advising me.

In his judgment, Lord Justice Nourse said I had become very disillusioned with Mr Warren's management agreement, which I had signed in January 1988, and that, by June, I had formed the view that Frank and I would not be able to resolve our differences. After issuing my writ against Frank the following month, I had asked Ambrose to act as my agent and advise on my career.

The judge commented that, thereafter, Mendy's activities included introducing commercial opportunities to me. He said Frank Warren had then started proceedings against Mendy, seeking injunctions and claiming that he had induced me to break the management agreement.

What was important in his judgment was the recognition by the Lord Justice that the trade of a professional boxer was a very specialist one. He said it required dedication, extensive training and expertise and that the boxer's professional life was short. The judge accepted that a high degree of mutual trust and confidence was required between boxer and manager.

However, even more important aspects arose from the case, which affected British boxing and the British Boxing Board of Control. The judges invited the BBBC to look at situations where a manager also holds a promoter's licence.

Lord Justice Nourse said it might be of advantage to the fighter in some circumstances but not in others. The judges clearly saw the dangers of one person having too much control over a fighter's career.

John Morris, who was then general secretary of the BBBC, said the board would consider changing its regulations. He said the stewards had, in the past, tried to separate the job of manager and promoter but were voted down by the licence holders. None of this would affect Ambrose, however, as he did not hold a licence and could not act in an official capacity. After the case, Frank said he would continue his legal fight and his lawyer told the judges that we had won the battle but not the war. After this case the BBBC changed the standard manager–boxer contract.

I had one more fight, to be held in Scotland, before my life would be turned upside down. Bagpipes heralded my entry to Glasgow. Ambrose had suggested I dress as the Tartan Terror to promote the bout against Mbayo Wa Mbayo from Zaïre. The French-based boxer was ranked number eight in Europe and was reckoned to be my toughest fight to date. Part of the proceeds were to go to the Lockerbie Disaster Appeal.

At the time, I was asked what I thought of my contemporaries in international boxing. Being me, I had plenty to say!

Herol Graham was, in my view, the perfect example of a second-rate fighter. He was just wasting his time hanging around for a title fight. I said he was not in the top drawer and that is why he wouldn't fight me.

Thomas Hearns was a legend, one of the all-time greats. I said I loved to watch him fight when I was a kid but I reckoned he would be about the easiest to beat because you can't go on forever, no matter how good you are.

Michael Watson was an interesting case — I was due to

fight him next after Mbayo. I asked if he could still make the weight as a middleweight. In all his fights he had weighed about 4lb over the limit but I said there was nothing more I wanted than to get in the ring with him.

Sumbu Kalambay — I said he was the best of the three world champions although he'd been around a long time without anybody taking much notice. He beat Herol by a mile when he was 30. I said if anyone wanted to call themselves a true world champion, he's the man they had to beat.

Iran Barkley — I fought him in America but, before then, I thought he was probably the strongest middleweight in the world. However, even though he was the WBC champion, I believed he was the weakest of the world's leading fighters in the division. He had knocked Tommy Hearns spark out, but the way his chin was then, so could anybody. Barkley's weakness was that he wasn't much of a technician.

Roberto Duran I rated for his achievements. He was an idol to so many young fighters and was still going for another world title at the age of 37. He was one of the most feared opponents in the world.

Michael Nunn was to be a future opponent and was then possibly one of the best middleweight fighters. I said at the time that he deserved to be IBF champion because he was such a good all-round fighter and the fittest middleweight in the world. He was a bit of a rarity in that he could punch as well as box.

The fight at Kelvin Hall, Glasgow, on 28 March, received less publicity than the excitement it generated over my coming match with Michael Watson. Some people were even saying it should not go ahead because of the small chance that I might not win. Mickey Duff, Watson's manager, had a get-out clause if I lost to Mbayo and, with my share of the purse amounting to £150,000,

Top left: I always make time for Timmy Mapother – one of my biggest fans! Timmy is a paraplegic who I met at a charity party – now we are great friends.
Top right: Many people claim to have 'made' Nigel Benn – but the only people who can claim to have done that are my parents, Mina and Dickson.
Above: Taking a break from the rigours of my training schedule.

Top: With Dominic and Sadé in my first cabriolet Porsche 911.
Inset; My wonderful children Conor, Sadé, Dominic, Renée and India, on Carolyne and my wedding day
Bottom: Me with Dominic (the fastest Playstation-player in the West), my beautiful daughter Renée and my Carolyne, the woman who has brought new meaning into my life.

Top: Sporting heroes! Me with Manchester United star, Teddy Sheringham.
Bottom: Me with a kissogram girl at my birthday party in January 1991. I was 'molested' by several ladies that night.

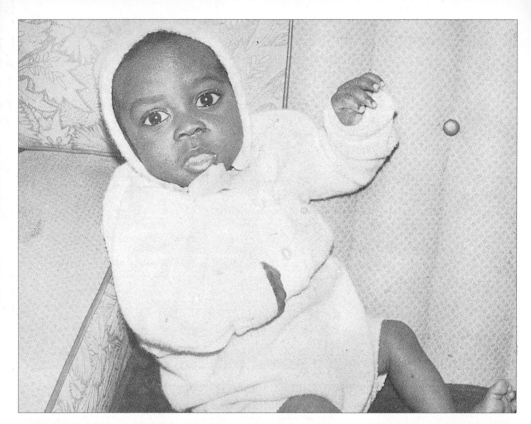

Top: The baby who grew to be world champion, still in nappies at the family home in Henley Road, Ilford, Essex.
Bottom: I cook my family's dinner most evenings. Here I am picking up a few tips from celebrity chef Ainsley Harriot.

1. The Dark Destroyer collects an award for best overseas boxer at a celebration banquet in Las Vegas. I'm pictured here with Tommy 'Hitman' Hearns, USA middleweight champion boxer who was rated No.2 in the world in 1987.

2. With Evander Holyfield.

3. With Mike McCallum, Jamaican world-rated heavyweight.

4. With Butch Lewis, a well-known USA promoter.

5. With Jeff Fenech, three times world champion bantam weight.

6. My idol: Marvin Hagler.

7. Floyd Paterson in London with me. He came over for the Lennox Lewis fight in 1992.

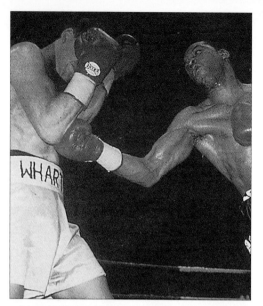

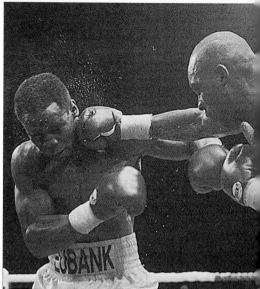

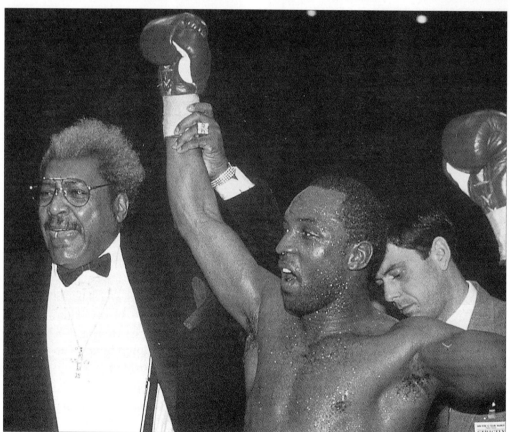

Top left: Fighting Henry Wharton, a challenger for my WBC super-middleweight belt at Earl's Court, London on February 26, 1996.

Top right: The one that got away. I still think I won a 'moral' victory in the controversial draw with Eubank in Manchester on October 9, 1993.

Below: With Don King, after I defeated Henry Wharton.

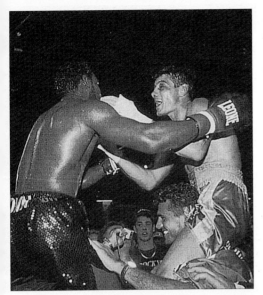

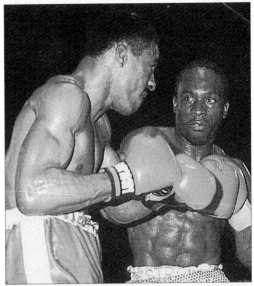

Top left: I won my second world title belt off the Italian Mauro Galvano in just three rounds. The Italian fans displayed bad manners by hissing and booing after my fight. It won me the prestigious WBC super-middle weight belt. The fight was staged in Marino, Italy on Ocober 3rd, 1992.

Top right: The Benn–Watson fight at Finsbury Park, London May 21, 1989 – my first, devastating defeat.

Bottom: With my proud Dad at Muswell Hill in London, April 20, 1988 after winning the Commonwealth middleweight title against opponet Abdul Umaru Sanda. The referee stopped the fight in the second round.

Top: In the army in 1982, with my brother John at Minden, West Germany, where we served with the Royal Regiment of Fusiliers. With mates (from left) Bodger, Maggie, John Benn and me.
Bottom: Another party at Jacqueline's Nightclub in Wardour Street. From left to right: Big John the Minder, me, Dermot Benn, Carl Russel, Phillip Chen, Donvean Thompson and John Benn.
Inset: Me in my army boxing kit.

there was a lot to lose.

However, I had promised to go ahead with the Glasgow fight and didn't want to let down the Lockerbie Disaster Appeal. Nor did I have the slightest doubt that I would beat my opponent. When we got into the ring he took what was coming. You can tell a lot by a man's hands and eyes. His hands were like granite. Rough, hard-working hands, the hardest hands I had ever felt in my life. He had come to fight but, looking at his eyes, I knew I would win.

I took him out in two rounds. My last punch actually lifted him off his feet and he ended up half out of the ring.

After-fight parties were virtually obligatory as a release from all the pre-fight tension and after-fight 'high'. The Glasgow whorehouse hired by Ambrose for partying following the Mbayo fight was one of the more memorable evenings. All my close buddies, like Rolex Ray, had flown up for the fight and had already tasted the exotic offerings this brothel had made available during the day. Ray, always the big spender, had parted with £1,500 before the party had even begun. The premises were normally used as a sauna and massage salon.

I was feeling pretty good having knocked out Mbayo in two rounds, so I wasn't exhausted. I don't know if it was Ray or Ambrose who organised it but, on our arrival at the brothel, a live sex show was immediately staged. Three girls stripped off their clothes until they were entirely naked and then put on a lesbian act for us. We were then invited to join them in a group orgy. Few refused. Ambrose had brought along his teenage son to initiate him into the ways of the world, although I don't think he personally took part in any of the activities.

After the live show, we played music, drank more champagne and for those who wanted more, and a lot of my mates did, about 20 girls were available for sex at a reasonable rate. As the night drew on, things got pretty wild and, at one stage, Rolex Ray did some rude things to a lady using her stiletto heel.

One of the people who were there told us he got more than he bargained for and returned home with a 'social' disease which he would have to explain to his lady. We were there until about 6.00am and I doubt if the girls would have been able to cope with going to work the next day.

The partying was good, but it was secondary. Now, finally, with 22 fights under my belt, I felt ready for Michael Watson. Until I fought him, only two men, Winston Burnett and Reggie Miller, had lasted beyond the second round. I had reached another turning point in my life.

11

MAY DAY

If Ambrose Mendy could have had his own way, I would have been a legend by lunchtime and a boxing deity by dinner. If he had had a war cry, it would have been 'Gimme a gimmick — as many as possible'. He was as economical with the truth as he was generous with bullshit but, somehow, his outrageous hype caught the imagination and both the press and television were happy to come along for the ride, until it all went sour.

At 25, I had the world at my feet. I had everything a young man could ever wish for — fame, fast cars, a beautiful woman, two children, property and thousands of adoring fans. As undefeated Commonwealth middleweight champion, I had 22 wins under my belt and Michael Nunn had made an offer of £2 million to fight me. On the home front, I was besieged almost daily by the media who were clamouring for interviews in the run-up to my fight with Michael Watson on 21 May 1989, at Finsbury Park, London.

Mendy's marketing skills, learned in prison, were a tribute to that institution. Love him or hate him, he did the job brilliantly, and I had never earned as much money before. The World Sports Corporation (Ambrose's grandly named company), which was really a one-man-band, used a motto which pleased as it teased: 'You ain't seen nuthin yet'. Now it went into overdrive to publicise my next fight.

Ambrose was master of the oral grand slam. He announced that everyone from Benny Hill, Page Three girls, Bob Geldof, Paula Yates, Engelbert Humperdinck and a host of other stars and sporting personalities had already bought tickets for the Benn–Watson fight to be held in a 'supertent' at Finsbury Park. Ambrose was never happier than when he held the floor and imagined he was manipulating the proceedings.

I went along with my guru's 'Benn's Bad' image. Lecturing to the eager journalists, Mendy agreed that style was more important than substance and added, 'The first thing to create is brand awareness. We are about Nigel Benn the name rather than Nigel Benn the boxer.' He boasted, 'I was the first to see the importance of brand awareness in boxing and, in general, I see sport as a stall for your goods.'

He claimed that all 7,000 tickets to the fight had been sold although this was a little wide of the mark. Ambrose made sure my name was never out of the news. One day he leaked the story that my fists had been insured for £10 million at an annual cost of £35,000. Another day, my £60,000 white Carrera Turbo Cabriolet Porsche 911 had increased in value to £120,000. Mendy claimed someone had offered to buy it from me for that price.

Posters of me shaking my fist with the words 'Michael, I'm Bad and You Know It' were posted all round London. This backfired a little as police and local authorities were becoming concerned over security arrangements at the tent in case fans were whipped up into a fighting frenzy. The British Boxing Board of Control said they were watching the situation closely.

With all the non-stop hype, Ambrose was publicly criticised by Frank Maloney, my promoter. He said, 'They try to outshine the boxers when they really only work for them.'

Ambrose would hold court at the Phoenix Apollo restaurant in Stratford which had become known as the local for the 'black pack', a group which included successful sportsmen. The name was a misnomer, however, as we were not all black. Members of this high-earning group included John Barnes, Vinny Jones, Linford Christie, Chris Waddle, Garth Crooks, Michael Thomas, Cyril Regis, Laurie Cunningham, David Rocastle, John Fashanu and Paul Davies. Mendy would inevitably arrive late for meetings and make a grand entrance so that all eyes would be on him. Our photographs, dominated by a large central one of Ambrose, gave us celebrity status on the restaurant walls.

Some of our group would also meet in the West End, usually at Brown's nightclub, and be ushered to the VIP room upstairs which was frequented by pop superstars like George Michael and Elton John.

If we had it, we flashed it. I showed off my gold bracelets and my £21,000 watch which, to the surprise and initial consternation of the shop manager, I had paid for in cash. He thought he was going to be mugged when I reached into my pocket for a wad of notes. Pictures were taken of me in my designer clothes. Encouraged by Ambrose, I was now spending £5,000 a month on clothes for myself, Sharron and the kids.

Around this time, an offer of $3 million was made by Michael 'Second To' Nunn, the International Boxing Federation champion, to fight me but we rejected it out of hand. Nunn was my age and had just knocked out World Boxing Association champion Sumbu Kalambay in 88 seconds in Las Vegas. He was undefeated in 33 fights, 23 of them inside the distance. Ambrose told the press that the American could stick his offer. I would continue fighting for British and European titles before thinking about the World Championship, and by the time I got around to him, his offer would be $5 million.

Magazines were invited into my home and photographs taken of my £10,000 stereo, the Porsche, the jewellery and an Italian-designed oasis of plastic trees which would light up above our double bed. I was described as being a 'real-life Rocky'.

Variations of the 'Dark Destroyer' tag were also applied to me: 'Rambo', 'The Mean Machine', 'The People's Champion', 'Mr Punch'. Ambrose's philosophy was the more, the merrier. Another name could mean another bum on a seat, another ticket, a bigger purse. All news was good news. Yesterday's news, like yesterday's blues, would soon be forgotten. Ambrose hinted to the press that over the next few years I would earn £10 million and they loved quoting big figures.

The boxing writers were also having a field day. My style was described as being what the Americans wanted: 'Vicious, clinical winner ... Benn is their kind of fighter, but in embryo, a man with natural gifts who knows that he needs a bit more study before going for broke.' They said I had been: '... brilliantly marketed and promoted — so much so, the Americans have suddenly woken up to the fact there's a second Big Benn in Britain.'

Just ten days before the fight, I was being lined up for a £1 million showdown with middleweight Mike McCallum, the new WBA champion, after he got a split decision against Herol Graham at the Albert Hall that month. However, the offer hinged on me beating Michael Watson.

The boxing experts were hedging their bets (mostly in favour of me) over the outcome of the fight, although all payed homage to my punching capacity. One wrote, 'The Benn punch is a phenomenon which happens maybe on six occasions in a lifetime. Backed up by other qualities it makes for an outstanding champion, a Mike Tyson for instance.'

But Michael Watson, who is a good friend, was not to be dismissed. Respected boxing writer Colin Hart, who matched us evenly, predicted a sixth-round win for Michael and told his *Sun* readers it might be worth a 7-1 punt on Michael. Watson had more experience than me but even so I was the 3-1 on favourite with the bookies while Michael's odds were 9-4. To win inside the distance I was 2-1 on and Michael 7-1. Former champions Alan Minter, Tony Sibson, Terry Downes and Herol Graham selected me to retain the Commonwealth title.

My trainer Brian Lynch still wouldn't let me do much sparring before the fight and, on hindsight, that may have been a mistake. He said, 'Nigel would have liked to but I wouldn't — and don't — let him do much. He's not getting in there having the life bashed out of him ... you don't need to be walloped all the time.'

Others were not sure that this was a good idea and said so. Colin Hart remarked, 'There's a tremendous contrast in the way these two have prepared for their £300,000 battle. Benn has sparred only 12 rounds in training, while Watson will have done nearly 60 when he winds up today.

'Surely no fighter on earth can learn to avoid blows unless he gets the right sparring practice? It's a method that has been used by boxers from great champions to novices — from Johnny L Sullivan's time to the present day.

'Lynch may well be right, but I have a feeling the trainers who look after the likes of Joe Louis, Robinson, Ali, and Leonard would violently disagree.'

Michael had also been training with Rod Douglas, whom I had beaten as an amateur to win the ABA championship.

My fight with Michael was the biggest of my life. There were 8,000 people in the tent at Finsbury Park and all the razzmatazz was beginning to affect me. I was over the moon at the £150,000 purse. It was the most I had ever been paid. However, in spite of all the hype, I always respected Michael's ability. He was a good boxer with a superb boxing brain and he had more experience than me. I thought I would stop him but it turned out to be the other way.

I had been locked away from my family in preparation for the fight and the day before the bout I wanted to change my hairstyle. I had extensions put in and then had it all pulled back so tight it stretched my whole face. I became so slant-eyed that it would only need buck teeth for me to look like the first black Chinese in the ring.

I entered the arena with all the glitz and glamour of a movie star. I'd told Michael Watson I was bad, and I was looking badder than ever. Michael, though, looked twice my size, built like a brick shithouse. I thought, 'It's do or die here.' Michael was looking cool and collected; I was giving it *large*, the Charley big potatoes.

We started eyeballing each other, and I became convinced that he couldn't manage me. I didn't think he was good enough to fight me — not in the same league. When the bell went for round one, I thought 'This is it, let's get started,' and went for him hammer and tongs. I was throwing big bombs, trying to explode on his chin. I kept on blasting him, but he was covering up well and this went on for three rounds. All of a sudden I said to myself, 'Fucking hell, nothing's happening!'

Then, at the start of the fourth, he connected with a whole bunch of head shots that had me on the ropes. I was in real trouble. The guy was taking all my best shots and was still smiling at me, saying, 'Come on, Nigel!' I couldn't understand it, I really couldn't. I thought I'd had it in the bag, but the man had sussed me.

Then, in the fifth, I heard my trainer call out, 'Go on, Nige! Steam him!' Steam him?

How do you do that, I thought. That's not in any of the

boxing pamphlets.

'Go in there, mate, get in there and steam him!'

Well, I tried, but in the sixth, I realised I was all burned out. I had nothing left and he floored me with a sharp jab. I just lay there watching the ref count me out, and it was at that moment that I realised I wasn't invincible. I'd lost my Commonwealth title, and I just thought, What am I going to do?

After losing to Michael Watson, I cried my eyes out. It was like having the whole world on my shoulders. A horrible, horrible experience. I was angry with those around me and my whole future, my world, crumbled before my eyes. With all the build up, the adoration, the adulation, defeat was even harder to take. There was an emptiness, a dark void. It was as if I had finished building the Canary Wharf skyscraper the previous day, only to see it crashing to the ground the next. I was utterly devastated.

Brian Lynch's public criticism of me didn't help either. He said, 'Nigel is stark, ravin' bonkers ... We had the simplest plan, but Nigel threw it out of the window — I screamed and pleaded with him in the corner but he just did the opposite. He certainly daren't go on taking the kind of head punches Watson caught him with. There's no doubt we are going to have to do a lot of work on his defence. When it became obvious he wasn't going to get Watson's chin, he should have switched his attack to the body to bring Michael's hands down.'

To this day, I don't know what Lynch meant by 'Steam him, Nige.' As I said, I couldn't find it in any of the manuals and I think he would have done better to keep his comments to himself. I was upset and humiliated, but Michael deserved praise for what he had done. I paid the price for making mistakes. Every time I threw a punch, Michael seemed to know it was coming and countered me.

My brother John said, 'I knew Nigel would lose after

round one. At that time, he had built such a reputation he was playing too much to the crowd. There was too much of the "I can knock out anybody" syndrome. A lot of that I put down to Ambrose. And his hairstyle didn't help in the least. It contributed a lot to his face swelling up because his skin was pulled back so tightly. It was all done for image and was totally unnecessary. In addition to that, he'd spent four hours in a chair having his hair plaited.' I suppose he was right. A lot of things contributed to my defeat that night — maybe my image was one of them.

Michael said he had respected me so much that he had trained like a maniac. 'I expected Nigel to make an explosive start but never realised just how fast he is. I felt the power of his punches on my gloves and I knew I couldn't take the risk of dropping my guard for a second. I knew I had to bide my time and, although I was dazed for a moment in the third round, I never let him land a clean shot on my chin. I did resent it that Nigel was getting all the publicity when I knew I was the better man. But I've got to hand it to him that, without Nigel and his image, I wouldn't have got this fight or the fortune that goes with it.'

Mickey Duff offered me advice for a comeback. Out would go my flamboyant management led by Ambrose Mendy; out would go trainer Brian Lynch's revolutionary approach to training based on a minimum of sparring; out would go the Hollywood-Rocky-style razzmatazz on big-fight nights. He also said he wouldn't let me fight for six months.

For my part, there were only two things I could have done: pack in boxing or start again. I thought long and hard and decided that losing was not going to be the end of the world, despite how I felt at the time, and that other people had lost and bounced back to become world champions. This is what I would do. Furthermore, it had become apparent that my previous victories, because they had been so decisive, had given me a limited round experience in the ring. That would now change.

Ambrose was not to be thwarted. The day after my defeat, he announced that my next fight would be in America in September and that American TV were sufficiently impressed by my defeat to feature my comeback. He said they would put up the money for me to meet a top-ten-rated fighter.

The news didn't lighten my burden. I knew it would be a long, hard slog back to the top. Yet, in a way, it was a blessing in disguise. It brought me firmly back to earth with one gigantic thud!

12

MIAMI

Defeat had weighed heavily on me and I was still licking my wounds after the Watson fight as I settled into my suite at the Doral Hotel at the end of July 1989. Miami smelled good. This was my first day and the palm trees, pools and tropical heat were uplifting. They softened the empty feeling in my stomach, brought on by this self-imposed exile away from my family and friends. I knew my destiny was here. This was going to be the springboard for my comeback.

My thoughts were thousands of miles away when the telephone rang. 'Nobody knows I'm here,' I thought, puzzled. Who could it be? The voice was husky and borrowed heavily from the casting couch technique. 'Hello,' it purred. 'I saw you come in.' There was a deep sigh, and the voice continued with a soft growl, 'I like you. I want to make love to you. I want to do things to make you tremble ...'

My face lit up. A cheerful grin spread slowly from ear to ear. My eyes sparkled. Hey, this sounds like fun. I've not even been here five minutes and somebody's already got my number and is doing the chat. Must be the gear I'm wearing. Americans like style. This lady's impressed. Things ain't going to be so bad after all!

The voice got steamier and the suggestions more obscene. 'What's all this about?' I asked, getting more interested by the second. I invited the caller to come up to my room.

The voice changed. 'I can't. You might not like what you see.'

The penny dropped. I suddenly realised the voice belonged to a bloke. My horny admirer was gay! I shouted out for a friend of mine: 'Graham, Graham!'

I was panicking. Everything happens in America. Something was going on here and I didn't like it. I wanted Graham to get me out of there. If this geezer came up I was going to throw him off the sixth-floor balcony.

The door to my suite opened and I was fuming. I was totally on edge. As far as men were concerned, I was a virgin and aimed to stay that way. The voice walked in. He was the hotel waiter. I'd never seen a black guy dolled up the way he was. His nails were more manicured than Princess Di's, he had a gold tooth and bounced along with a dainty step. I was ready to give it to him but definitely not where he wanted. I was going to gouge out his eye and mash his head. But he was so friendly and cheerful that, once he saw the situation was hopeless, we got on really well. He then filled up the mini-bar and said, 'I just put that in there for free,' and began telling me about his conquests. I didn't want to know that he found his black lovers too coarse and rough!

Ambrose had also come to Miami to settle me in and speak to promoters. He'd tried to cheer me up and help me to get over my post-Watson blues. Immediately after the fight, we had travelled to Jamaica for a week to attend the International Boxing Federation conference. Ambrose was his outrageous self and nearly got us involved in a fight with a taxi driver who looked like a tough Yardie. He'd asked for more than $20 for the fare, and Ambrose gave him less, and said, 'Take it or leave it, you ain't getting no more,' and took his shirt off. He was ready to fight for his principles. However, when the cabby called his bluff by removing his own shirt, Ambrose began talking his way out of it. He tried scaring the guy by telling him that we were both top boxers with the IBF and, fortunately for him, it worked.

The taxi driver said he was not going to fight another black man and backed down. Had he wanted to do so, however, he could have torn Ambrose apart. And I would have loved nothing better than seeing Ambrose prance around like Sugar Ray Leonard. We had a good week out there and I remember going sunbathing on the beach and later wondering what the hell I was doing it for when I already had a good tan. After lying in the sun, I looked blacker than the ace of spades.

After the Watson fight, I'd spent a week in the West Indies, and coming back to London was painful. I had to live with the constant reminder of my defeat as I gathered together my belongings and packed for Miami. I would be starting a new life and saying goodbye to Sharron and my kids so that I could concentrate on my comeback in the USA.

I told the press that I was going back to basics and turning away from all distractions to put myself on course for the world title. I told them I had been a real wally and fought like a berk against Michael Watson, but now I had learned a lot about myself and was so disgusted with watching my performance on television that I didn't want to be seen outdoors. It was like a nightmare haunting me. I needed to learn to move differently, fight more rhythmically and work out how to handle clever boxers like Watson. Out would go the hangers-on around me and the jet-set lifestyle and other temptations to which I had always been so partial.

Brian Lynch could have taken part in my comeback but he chose not to come to America with me. To improve technichally, I wanted someone with more experience in the ring than him. He could join me as my trainer to condition me but I wanted Vic Andreeti, who lived in Miami, to train me in fighting techniques. Vic, who was also from the East End of London, was the undefeated British light welterweight champion in the Sixties and had emigrated to America. He could also provide top sparring partners for me at Fifth Street gym in Miami where boxing greats like Muhammad Ali, Joe Louis and Sonny Liston had trained.

A week before I left, Ambrose was charged with conspiring to defraud banks and financial institutions. This was one more nail in the coffin that would eventually drive us apart.

When we left, I was like a dog with its tail between its legs. I had to make a fresh start and I was determined to put everything I had into training. I was convinced I had more to offer. Nigel Benn, trained soldier, would kick ass again. I had more ambitions to fulfil and one defeat was not going to make me stop. As I said, my loss may well have been a blessing in disguise. Had I gone on to beat Michael I might have messed things up with a world title. Now I was at at a major crossroads in my career.

The stardom and fame had happened too quickly. It was time to get off the merry-go-round. Vic Andreeti got down to business immediately and all the big boys came down to Miami. I liked the way they did business out there. They didn't recognise defeat. No Eddie the Eagles were permitted to crash-land here. They wanted winners.

I rented an apartment in Collins Avenue on Miami Beach. It was millionaire's row. Behind me was Julio Iglesias' house and nearby Gloria Estefan's sprawling manor which made my place look like a cardboard box. An English couple I got to know out there, Pat and Pete, befriended me and looked after me over the three years I was there. When I moved into the Carnage Club, a very classy place with lots of wealthy tenants, a Jewish lady asked me to carry her bags from her car. I had to explain to her politely that I was not a porter. I would still turn heads in Miami. Not because they recognised me as a boxer but because I looked the part in my Armani suits and designer clothes and Americans appreciated that.

Although I had the best of intentions when I told the British press I would be living the life of a monk out there, I wasn't lonely for too long after my arrival and my prediction of a quiet life was a little wide of the mark. My mate Rolex Ray unexpectedly turned up. He'd had a few problems in England and went to live in Spain for a couple of months. While there he met up with The Who and accompanied them to Miami for a concert. He phoned Sharron in London to ask about me and was told I was in Miami. By coincidence, he could see my hotel from his and, within ten minutes of calling Sharron, he was in my room. We ended up staying together for a while until Ray got his own apartment. Ray joined me in some of my training sessions and he and I would go for early morning runs along the beach.

Running before dawn involved some risk. Helicopters would come zooming down, training their spotlights on us to identify who we were. There was so much drug smuggling along that section of beach that everyone was a suspect until they got to know you. One of our friends once found a load of drugs washed up on the sand and, thereafter, would organise his runs according to the time of the tides.

I was training really hard, at least three times a day. The morning runs would be about five to six miles along South Beach. Ray would do about four miles and then we'd go to the gym at lunchtime. At about five or six in the evening, we'd go to the health club at the Hilton.

Afterwards, we'd wine and dine at the top restaurants and clubs. There was a very good club scene in Miami and we took full advantage of it. When Ray came over with The Who, we took John Entwhistle to Stringfellows where I met a beautiful waitress called Lois Harrington. Later, she sold her story to the press and told them I'd eaten strawberries and cream off sensitive parts of her body. As a result, boxing writer Colin Hart delivered some strawberries and cream just before my comeback fight against Jorge Amparo in Atlantic City on 20 October, and said he believed it was a necessary part of my training and diet!

Apart from Ray staying with me for a while, Terry Marsh also came over before he was arrested on suspicion of shooting Frank Warren, and the three of us shared the same flat for a while. In fact, when Terry and I flew back together to England, he was arrested after going through Customs. I'd been with him and one moment he was there, the next he'd gone. I didn't know what had happened. I thought he'd been hauled off by Customs over his duty-free allowances.

Terry was a laugh-a-minute while he was in America. When we went to Atlantic City he had everyone in fits of laughter with his antics. Once, Ambrose bought us (with my money!) ski-type all-in-one striped suits. They were in matching colours and we had just arrived at the airport and were waiting for our luggage when Terry went missing. The rest of us — Ambrose, Ray, Vic Andreeti and I — looked everywhere for him without success. All of a sudden, we saw this figure wearing the same suit as us, curled up on the luggage carousel. It was Terry. He'd rolled himself into a ball, pulled up the hood on his ski suit and was going round and round with the luggage. He kept his head down and looked just like a package. It was the funniest thing you'd ever seen. But apart from getting up to tricks like this, he was very much a loner.

America was a crazy place. Once, in Las Vegas, we saw one lady who acted as a pimp for her daughter. The girl was only about 16 but very pretty and the mother tried to pair her up with me thinking she might get a few bob out of it.

On another night in Vegas, we met Tyson. I was with Ray and Ambrose in a black club. Tyson was sitting alone but recognised me from the television. Ray asked him if he could have a photograph taken with him and he declined saying he didn't have photos done with white guys. 'They're pussies,' he told him. Ray said he ought to feel his stomach before making statements like that. He took it as an invitation to test his muscles and hit him. I think it really hurt but he was only playing around.

We saw him later with six or seven girls and, judging from the way he was carrying on with them, it seemed clear that if Tyson were to ask anyone back with him they would know without any doubt what was going to happen. Every woman who comes up and asks for a kiss or autograph gets asked if he can touch her pussy. He would grab every girl within reaching distance. We had a good laugh with him but he is so powerful and intimidating.

While in Miami, I met a dancer who was with an all-girl group. She was really sexy and the first time I made love to her I thought I was going to die. It was explosive! We walked along the beach talking about all the sexy things she would like to do. I said, 'Here's your man!' That was it. She began taking off all my clothes and wouldn't let me do a thing. She was an older woman with a beautiful body. We made love on the sand but were taking a hell of a risk because if the police had seen my black ass bobbing up and down they'd have arrested us.

On one of my trips back to London from Miami I chatted up an air stewardess and we tried to make love on the seat of the aircraft. Her boyfriend, a steward, found out and threatened to do me when we landed.

Ambrose and Ray got on well but were never great buddies. Ray knew Ambrose from Jody's, a club in Spitalfields Market, east London, where he said a lot of trendy villains would go. The doorman, Roy Shaw, a bare-knuckle fighter, was one of the toughest bouncers in London. Ray was about 18 at the time and Ambrose was about to go to prison for fraud, where he shared a cell with a good friend of Ray's.

While Ray thought Ambrose was clever and impressive, he was not too keen on his methods. He warned me, 'Ambrose was always around black sportsmen. He had lots of charisma, talked well and got into their family, becoming godfather to the children. By the time they got wise to him, it was often too late.'

In spite of my nights out, I trained with a new zeal and dedication. Vic Andreeti had calmed me down in the ring and showed me how to feel my way with a jab and to defend myself properly. He said I was '... all crash, bang, wallop, but he's listening and showing me an absolutely lovely left jab'. At the same time Ambrose and I had talks with Bob Arum in New York, who was interested in signing me up for a fight deal. Arum said he had watched me fight Watson on TV and thought I was the most exciting middleweight he'd seen in years. He wanted to feature me on the undercard at a coming fight in Las Vegas between Sugar Ray Leonard and Roberto Duran. We signed a two-fight deal with Top Rank, Bob's promotion company, on 29 August. I was on trial. If I did well in the two fights, I would be in line to fight a world title. If I lost, I'd be finished.

My début fight in America was to be against Jorge Amparo at the International Hotel in Atlantic City on 20 October 1989. Amparo, a 35-year-old veteran, had been the distance with four world champions and had never been on the floor. Shortly before the fight, panic set in. I had a health scare and was losing up to ten pounds in every training session. After extensive medical tests, I was told that my training had been too intensive and that I had sapped my body fat to dangerously low levels. Vic kept telling me to take it easy in the amount of training I was doing but I wouldn't let up. The doctor told me that if I went into the ring in this state, I was risking serious injury and even putting my life at risk. The doctors at Miami Sports Clinic told me to rest and fill myself with carbohydrates, which did the trick and got me back into A1 condition.

Sparring with top-class fighters had also done wonders for my confidence. In three months I had learned more than in the previous three years. Freddie Pendleton, a world-class boxer, taught me to stay cool and pick my punches. I also learned to pace myself and not go hell for leather like I did against Watson. I used to go out and try to blow away my opponent and wouldn't listen to a word anyone said before the next round when I would carry on in exactly the same way. That had all changed.

In the three months I was away, I was missing my family and Sharron and the kids terribly and made up my mind to return to England immediately after my fight. During my absence I had spent thousands of dollars on phonecalls to Sharron and had even considered marriage to her the following year, but right now the most important thing was to win.

When they put me in the ring with Jorge, I took one look at him and thought they'd put me in the ring with an animal. He was tough. No boy this one. He was a grown man. This guy had fought with the top men — the real McCoy. I instantly realised that winning this fight was going to be worth all my previous victories put together. It's not until you step into the ring with fighters like

Amparo that you find out how good you are. And especially for me, because I knew that if I lost this fight I was finished. I was more scared of losing than of anything else.

In the first round I was banging away, but I knew I had to be careful not to tire myself out. I had to make a good impression, so I was jabbing and hitting, but my hand kept bouncing of his head. At one point, I flung myself back on the ropes, and then threw myself forward, punching him in the head. I hit him so hard I thought he would be out cold. It felt like my hand had shattered, but the guy just shook his head and took it.

The fight went the full ten rounds, and I got a conclusive win on points. Afterwards, I remember crying with relief. This win meant I had my foothold in America, but it also made me realise I had a lot to learn. If I'd had that fight a year earlier, I'd have been knackered after the sixth round. But now the Dark Destroyer was back on the world stage.

After the fight, I returned to England and was back with Sharron. It was great being back with her and Dominic and Sadé. We were one, big happy family, reunited after my absence. After being separated from them for three months, I realised how important it was for me to have the family. But it was also important to be able to provide for Sharron and the kids and that meant concentrating on my next fight.

During my short visit home, I was invited to appear on the *Kilroy* programme to discuss whether boxing encouraged violence in youngsters. Ironically, Ambrose, who had come to join me, was involved in a scrap outside the BBC's Lime Grove Studios in west London. His car nearly collided with another vehicle and the two drivers had something to say about it. The police were called but no charges were brought.

I predicted a one-round victory for my second US fight. My opponent was Jose Quinones, a tough Puerto Rican, and our bout was set for 1 December in Las Vegas. I said I would go out and crack him on the chin in the first round. I needed to do something a little dramatic for America to sit up and take notice. Back in Britain, a number of people, including Mickey Duff, were surprised I was taking on someone as tough as Quinones who had KO'd 20 of his 26 wins. I was feeling good, really fit and 100 per cent psyched for a victory. It was going to be a good Christmas.

I knew Quinones was tough. I'd seen him beat Errol Christie, and he'd flattened Doug De Witt. But I was cool about my fight with him, I felt good and relaxed, and I knew I wasn't going to waste a lot of shots on him. The fight took place at the Hacienda Hotel in Las Vegas.

People started calling me the English Hagler after my fight with Quinones. That was a bit over the top, but it was a good fight for me and I took him out in 170 seconds of the first round. My new fighting style was beginning to show — I just took my time and picked my shots well, using my jabs. When I caught him with an uppercut, I didn't realise how much I'd hurt him. There were a load of English fans in the audience, though, and when I heard how hard they were cheering, I looked into his eyes and saw they were rolling. Out, mate!

Victory meant that a world title was again within my reach, much closer than I had thought. My promoter Bob Arum wanted me to fight Mike McCallum in England the following February. But there was also a challenge for the new WBO title which Iran Barkley and Doug De Witt were contesting in January. Arum had complete faith in me. He said I was an exception to the usual image Americans had of British fighters. Over there, British boxers were not thought to be much good. I had shown otherwise. He said I could follow Sugar Ray Leonard and Roberto Duran who were the last of the great legends in boxing. I could be his man of the Nineties. He made me feel good.

After the fight, I had planned to return immediately to England but stayed on a few days in Las Vegas for the Sugar Ray Leonard–Roberto Duran fight. I wished I had come home earlier. Along with others, I left disgusted after the eleventh round. It was pathetic. Leonard held on to his WBC world super-middleweight title against Duran and I never felt so let down. That was the biggest disappointment for me. I'd been looking forward to the fight all week and it turned out to be boring rubbish.

Given the opportunity, I would have got in the ring with either of them. Duran put up a pathetic fight. He used to be a god among fighters, the most ferocious of them all. What a let down. I wanted it to be a proud moment in boxing. I was all keyed up and sitting with my idol Mike Tyson and showbusiness celebrities like Michael Jackson. I'd even bought a special suit and was looking really smart. But I might have as well come in a tracksuit and trainers. It taught me one thing — you have to know when to quit.

13

WORLD CHAMPION

W e called the Billionaire Boys Club the BBC. It was my idea to start this small and exclusive club with about five or six pals, all of whom had deep pockets and long arms and liked enjoying themselves. It is still going today although some of the faces have changed. Of the original club members, two of them are doing very long prison sentences, including 14 years for armed robbery, one is dead and another went off his head.

There are five of us now — Rolex Ray; Chris, a diamond broker; Geoff; Albert, a Chechen who lives in Moscow and was Soviet light-heavyweight boxing champion; and me.

We live life to the full, have been known to take over front-row seats at events and always insist on the best tables at clubs and restaurants. We drive the biggest cars and live like pop stars, or possibly even better, because we have the good fortune to conduct most of our activities with a degree of anonymity and so rarely get reported.

One of the boys once booked a yacht for the weekend for £12,000 and then flew us out to its Mediterranean berth by aeroplane. Once there, he ferried in some lady friends by helicopter and we enjoyed a millionaire's break. When the good times rolled, they really rolled. We once had a stretch limousine to take us partying to the Barbican Hotel and spent three days and three nights there with an unlimited supply of vintage champagne and classy ladies.

We always did things in style, no matter what our circumstances might have been at the time. Albert, who lives in Moscow, was brought over to Canada to box after becoming Soviet champion. He was only about 21 at the time and, when we met, he was with a group of Russian boxers in Miami who weren't getting much money while training for fights. Ray took Albert under his wing and became his manager. We called Albert 'Gucci man' because he was given $100 subsistence which was meant to last him one month and he spent it all on the first day on a $100 Gucci shirt.

He was a good fighter but, after the break-up of the Soviet Union, he returned to Grozny on the Caspian Sea. His father was an influential businessman and friend of the President. The next we heard of Albert was that he was living in Moscow and had two Mercedes 500SL convertibles and was worth pots of money. He'd made it big in banking and didn't bother returning to his architectural studies at a famous Moscow college. Since we became friends, he comes to all my fights and after-fight parties. The Chechens would like him to return home and become mayor of Grozny but he is presently recovering from some bullet wounds that he sustained while on a home visit.

Like the others, he has a great sense of humour, loves dance, techno and garage music and is a hit with the ladies. Once, he spent £40,000 in two days while courting a beautiful Israeli girl who works for a top jeweller. He and Ray met her in Stringfellow's where she was a bit stand-offish at first, but she soon became very much friendlier. Not so long ago, Albert brought over one of his Chechen friends and his five-year-old son. They went shopping in Harrods and Ray offered to buy the little boy a toy machine-gun. The lad cast it aside with contempt and his father had to explain to Ray that, back home, he owned a real machine-gun. Albert always said he loved the circus and pageantry involved in boxing as much as the sport itself. We trained together in Miami and he never forgot Ray's generosity to him.

I returned to London after my second victory to spend Christmas at home with Sharron and the children. It was great to see them all and one of the first things I did was to go on a shopping spree for some clothes. I spent £25,000 in less than half an hour. I wanted to look the part when I returned to America for my next fight against Sanderline Williams who'd been substituted for Michael Olajide at Atlantic City on 14 January. That fight was going to be one of my most important because a win would get me a chance at a title match.

All the boxers and stars I had met in the States dressed beautifully and I wasn't going to be outdone by them. I bought 20 suits, 30 pairs of shoes and 40 shirts as well as ties and belts. I could afford the money because I'd just signed a fresh five-fight deal with Bob Arum for £1.25 million.

Everything was being planned for a fight between me and Roberto Duran in London in May if certain obstacles could be overcome. Barry Hearn and his Matchroom organisation had linked up with Bob Arum to stage the fight but were having problems with the British Boxing Board of Control. Doubts had been expressed over Duran's fitness and Ambrose angrily announced that I would never again fight in Britain if the council prevented the bout from going ahead. I had been promised a purse of £650,000 if the fight took place, although it was dependent on me winning all my bouts in the States.

Other British boxers, including Herol Graham and Michael Watson, got the hump over the proposed match saying they were ahead of me in ratings and should therefore be given the opportunity to challenge for a world title ahead of me. After the Williams fight I was rated number 5 in the World Boxing Organisation, number 6 in the International Boxing Federation, number 7 in the World Boxing Association and number 9 in the World Boxing Council.

Liverpool-born Canadian Michael Olajide had to pull out of our fight because of a cut hand and I had to fight Williams who was from Cleveland and had gone the distance with Iran Barkley and Frank Tate and had never been knocked out. I had asked Sharron to come to the fight and made the mistake of looking for her in the crowds during the bout. In that brief distraction, Williams smacked me on the chin and knocked out my gumshield, so I told her not to come to future fights.

I beat Olajide on points, though, and was looking forward to being able to challenge Roberto Duran for his WBC title. I was really disappointed when I heard the news that the fight with Duran had fallen through. It would have been a big draw and the purse could have increased to £1 million.

The WBC had stripped him of his title because he didn't defend it within the required period. Roberto had until 24 January to appeal but nothing was heard from him. Instead, I challenged Doug De Witt for his World Boxing Organisation middleweight title in Atlantic City on 29 April.

John Morris, the secretary of the British Boxing Board of Control, said his organisation would not recognise me as champion if I won the title. He said, 'We do not recognise the WBO.'

My fight was to be part of a triple bill. George Foreman would be fighting Cuban Jose Ribalta and Hearns would defend against Michael Olajide.

I flew back to London with Terry Marsh and Ambrose, arriving at Gatwick on 17 January. That was when Terry was arrested and charged with Frank's attempted murder. I went with him when he was taken under escort to Hackney police station where a special squad interrogated him. We were both surprised and shocked at his arrest. A few days later, we were told that Ambrose Mendy's offices in Tower Bridge had been broken into and secret documents relating to Terry and me had been taken. Mendy said, 'Whoever did this knew exactly what they were looking for,' and claimed that boxing enemies had paid to have his offices ransacked.

One of my favourite London nightclubs at this time was Jacqueline's, run by David Simones. I used to go there at weekends to relax and listen to music, and I got pally with David who, as I said, became my agent. One of our favourite tricks was to do wheelies with my Porsche in Wardour Street. He claims I went through four clutches and two gearboxes in less than a year, but I think it was only three clutches. Dave said my wheelie was the longest he had ever seen in the West End.

We had lots of parties down at his club. Kissogram girls would be invited to my birthday celebrations and stag parties, and there were always Page Three girls among the fun crowd who frequented the Soho club. When David launched his Dream Girls dance troupe, I was at the club with Gazza, John Barnes, Gary Mason and a load of other top sporting personalities, as well as most of the cast of *The Bill* and *EastEnders*. Gazza and I tried to jump on stage and dance with the girls, but David stopped us.

Shortly before I was due to leave for Miami to train for the fight against Doug De Witt, an incident from the past reared its ugly head and I was attacked with ammonia which was squirted into my face as I parked my Porsche. The attacker ran off and I had to be helped to hospital. Thankfully, there was no permanent damage but I was temporarily blinded in one eye.

I knew who my assailant was. He was a former friend who, oddly enough, would become so again. At that time, however, if I'd tried to get even with him, our vendetta would have continued until one of us had been killed.

The problem arose over my cheque book which someone else had taken and this chap had somehow become involved. Friction was building up between us and, at one point, I considered shooting him but then decided that everyone would know it was me. It's just as well I didn't because he was the one who saved me when I reached a really low point in my life.

A great deal of pressure was being piled on me from every corner over the next fight. I had many detractors who were envious of the amount of publicity my fights were getting. There was jealousy from other British boxers who could not get a title fight and then there was pressure from my promoters. I not only had to win the next fight but I had to win it in style. It had to look spectacular, otherwise the paying public would not be interested in watching me fight on television. If I looked good, then future prize money could be measured in millions. Bob Arum was talking about setting up a fight with Tommy Hearns if I beat De Witt.

The British press were not too optimistic about my chances with De Witt and harped on about my defeat by Watson. Even Colin Hart, who'd accurately predicted the round in which I'd lose to Watson, thought I'd be out by the sixth round.

Doug De Witt, the man described as having an 'iron hand', said there would be no contest in the fight against me. 'Benn doesn't know what he's in for,' he said, 'because whichever way he wants to fight, I'm much better than him ... I should enjoy myself with Benn because he's definitely the world's most over-hyped fighter. He's going to have a war on his hands and it's going to be interesting to see his reaction when he discovers he can't hurt me.'

De Witt's career had been quite impressive. In 42 fights he had lost 6 and drawn 4 against high-class opponents. He sparred with Marvin Hagler when he was 18 and 7 years later became number 3 to the world champion. The fight was at Caesar's Palace in Atlantic City. What a run-down, seedy dump that town was. There were drug pushers and prostitutes on every corner. I hated the place. But that's where the fight was, so that's where I went.

De Witt was a serious fighter, but I knew he didn't have my determination and, as soon as I set eyes on him in the ring, I knew I was going to win. When you've got a world title within your grasp, it gives you the balls to give what it takes. He was a mean-looking man, though. The guy looked like he'd had his face kicked in by a mule. His nose had been broken and pushed flat, which made him look even more menacing. Before the fight started, De Witt walked over to me in the ring and said, 'You're going down.'

'I might be going down,' I replied, 'but you're *staying* down!'

And then the bell rang.

From the beginning of the first round, the punches were heavy, and it wasn't long before blood began to trickle from De Witt's left eye. I could see it was bothering him, which gave me all the confidence I needed. In the second round, I kept going for the cut. It was a real slugfest on both sides, punch after punch after punch. Suddenly, I found myself taking a left hook which put me on the floor. But even when he put me down it didn't hurt me — I stayed down until the ref counted eight, and then I was up again, hitting him with a big left hook. There were only a few seconds remaining in the round, and De Witt had lost his chance.

I carried on battering him all over the place throughout the next few rounds, bashing the granny out of him. When you have to cut down a big tree, you keep chopping away and eventually it will fall — you don't just knock it down with one blow. That's what it was like with De Witt. He went down in the eighth when I bashed him with a left hook and then a right — just to be sure. He fell to his knees, with his hands stretched out in front of him. The count went to nine before he struggled to his feet and took the hardest right uppercut I could muster before going down again. He hit the canvas for a third time in the round after a final left hook, and I knew he wouldn't be able to go on.

We both took some punishment that night. De Witt saved every punch with his face, and I'd bashed him round the ring and split both his eyes. His ear was so smashed up it had turned blue, and his trainer said it was the worst injury he'd ever seen in his life. I'd never seen a man take so much pain. After eight rounds, his body just couldn't take any more.

My eye was split as well, and had to be stiched up. I also broke my wrist with the very last punch of the fight. But, you know, I hardly thought about that — I was 25 years old and had just been declared WBO World Middleweight Champion. Now the sky was the limit.

A lot of people think that was my best fight. Bob Arum was delighted. 'I told you he was the British Marvin Hagler,' he told everyone.

It was a fantastic night for British boxing, too, even if the British Boxing Board of Control didn't recognise my WBO title. The secretary, John Morris, said afterwards, '... I take great pleasure in Nigel's victory and in fact have sent him a letter of warm congratulation. Personally, I am delighted by a result which is good for British boxing. However, the fact remains that we do not at the present time recognise the WBO ... Certainly Benn could defend his title here and the WBO could provide officials, if they were recognised as judges and referees by a commission we recognised, New Jersey, for instance. We aim to control firmly but I don't think public confrontation benefits anyone.'

But I didn't worry too much about that. The promotors and television executives and the fans — everyone who mattered — knew I was now a world champion. I wasn't the same fighter I had been with Watson. This had been the biggest fight of my life. It was make or break time and, had I lost, it would have been the end of me. Everyone had thought I was a coward when I lost to Watson. When I got knocked down then, I didn't want to get up again, but I did, even though I wasn't sure what to do. With this fight I had a totally clear head and when I went down I knew I had eight seconds to get myself together. Something else that pleased me was that the Americans who had laughed when Bob Arum described me as 'his English Hagler' would now have to eat their words. I returned home in style, on Concorde, so that I could see my kids before they were tucked up in bed.

14

FERRARI DAYTONA

Miami was a tough but beautiful place. There was no middle ground. You were either rich or poor and guns did a lot of the talking. As protection, although I never had use for it, I bought a 9mm Browning, the same kind of gun I had in the Army. I wish I'd had it with me when there was a showdown between a group of us and the driver of another car who fished out a sawn-off shotgun from under his seat and aimed it straight at me in the underground car park of a Miami nightclub. I dived to the floor and we sped off.

Later, I was involved in another fracas which could have come straight from a scene in *Miami Vice*. It happened when I was surrounded by half-a-dozen tall, gum-chewing cops at a Daytona garage. They were the size of American footballers and they looked mean. In fact, they had been expecting my personal manager Peter De Freitas instead of me.

I'd been well and truly stitched up by the garage in question. The TV series *Miami Vice* used three identical Ferrari Daytonas. One was used for stunts, another was to be blown up and a third was a regular run-about. I liked the stunt car, which had been used by actor Don Johnson, and bought it from Paramount studios. The garage had been commissioned to do some work on it and I paid them

$6,000 in advance, which should have covered the cost of the work. It was left there for quite a few months, during which time I fought in Las Vegas, returned to England and then came back to Miami to train.

By this time I had Peter De Freitas with me. Peter is a big man who was formerly my bodyguard and doesn't mince his words. As a young man he had been in trouble with the authorities and had experienced a tougher regime than most.

I shied away from him a little at first because I received anonymous letters saying he'd been a bad boy. But that was all history as far as I was concerned. Nevertheless, it was useful having somebody around who could take care of himself. I was owed £60,000 once and Peter telephoned the debtor and suggested he check him out and then either tell him to push off or pay the money. The next morning, we collected £60,000 in cash. Pete is not scared of my Dark Destroyer image, either. I was giving him a hard time once when I'd asked him to organise a birthday cake for Sharron. It was quite late in the afternoon when he brought it round and I said I didn't want it any more. Pete threw the cake at me and it splattered against the door of my apartment. The thought did cross my mind to slam him one but I was exhausted from training and he's a big bloke. I saw the funny side of the situation, wiped the cream off my door with a finger and said it tasted good.

Years later, we fell out. But at the time, I felt I could rely on Pete, so I asked him to sort out the Ferrari for me. I'd phoned a number of times and asked for the car to be returned and so had Pete. The garage was sitting on it and didn't bother returning our calls. Pete and I then went round to the garage and saw that very little work had been done on the car. On my instructions, Pete took the garage owner to one side and told him not to mess us about. 'Are you going to repair the car or not?' he asked. The owner, who'd told us a number of different stories, said he would do it but it was the same old story.

Then the next time Pete went round, he told him, 'I'll tell you what I'll do. I'll get another $6,000 out of the bank and I'll give it to one of them herberts in downtown Miami and he'll come down and sort you right out.'

Two days later a Miami detective was on the phone to Peter, accusing him of threatening behaviour with a gun. That was untrue — Peter didn't have a gun — but the detective became quite belligerent and threatened to lock him up. He said: 'You're in my country now, not yours. We were told you threatened the man with a gun and that you wore a shoulder holster at the time.'

I had used some threats down the phone myself and these had been recorded. I'd decided to take Sharron, Dominic and Sadé with me to collect the car, to show that I wasn't interested in any trouble. But none of us had expected such a full-on welcome committee. Any moment now, I thought, one of these guys is going to pull a gun and lock me up.

It turned out that the police had been tipped off in advance. I pretended that nothing had happened and tried to smooth relations by offering to pay a little extra for the work.

The garage owner said it would be another 12. That's a lot, I thought, but for the sake of peace I paid up $1,200. He turned to me, with the police standing around, and said, 'Keep it coming, twelve *thousand*.' There was no option but to pay up. I'm still angry about it. We had treated him with respect. If the police hadn't been around he'd have been eating through a straw for the next six months. They said the garage man could have sued us for threatening him and Pete had to leave the country for a while. The car's back here now. It's one of my favourites. If I hadn't paid up the money the police would have made sure the garage kept the car.

Before Pete's unscheduled departure, we'd had good times in Miami nightclubs. He was with me when we wandered by mistake into a gay bar and I had my bottom squeezed. Pete joked about it, saying, 'The guy who squeezed Nige's bottom was a lovely feller. Nigel can't remember his name but he made a lovely breakfast!' Pete learned that champagne can be a great aphrodisiac. He called a blonde over after she'd been watching him crack a bottle and she said what a good-looking feller he was. Next, her mate joined me and we made an interesting foursome. Pete borrowed my convertible jeep the next day to take his new friend to lunch and got soaking wet when he couldn't work out how to put the roof up.

One of our friends in Miami was Mickey Rourke. We went out a lot with him, especially to Thai Tony's. He was quite a fan of mine and used to train with me at the Fifth Street gym. We went with him to watch his fight in Fort Lauderdale, Miami. He had once tried to spar with me but had second thoughts when he realised what it might involve, especially when he saw me on the pads. We'd go out together after fights. He would wear jeans and drive his black Cadillac. He was a very down-to-earth guy but, with the greatest will in the world, I would never call him a brilliant fighter. People would boo him in the ring and he would scream 'Up yours' at them and give them the V sign. He fought in Tokyo as a super middleweight and, surprisingly, won most of his bouts. His childhood dream was to be a boxer and his acting has helped him to live out his fantasy. I respect him because he says what he thinks. He won't crawl to film directors or sleep with them for a part as one well-known boxer did.

One of the best things to happen to me was meeting my idols Marvin Hagler and Mike Tyson, as well as all the other top international boxers. This was at an awards ceremony in Las Vegas where I'd picked up an award as best overseas boxer. Sugar Ray Leonard and Tommy Hearns were also there. Marvin wanted me to meet his girlfriend and he came over and introduced her. I couldn't believe this was happening. It was great.

My broken hand delayed the defence of my new world title although another battle was gathering pace — my fight with the British boxing authorities. The *Times* reported on 1 May 1990 that, following my victory over De Witt, I was expected to be out of action for at least six weeks. It said, 'Since hands are not designed for battering human heads it is not surprising that after the ferocity of his non-stop attack on the American, Benn suffered such damage. Since heads are not made to be hit by human baseball bats, it is not surprising that De Witt, an old campaigner, announced his retirement from boxing immediately after the bout.'

The British Board of Boxing Control refused my WBO world title opponent Iran Barkley a licence to fight in Britain because of eye trouble. A defence had been planned on 18 August at Old Trafford, Manchester, and a minimum purse of $1 million had been guaranteed, although it was likely to be much higher. As a result, I would have to fight Barkley in Las Vegas. The incredible situation had arisen whereby the BBBC would not recognise me as a world champion, and they would not grant a licence to Barkley to fight me in England. Their decision cost me hundreds of thousands of dollars. Yet despite the non-recognition and the refusal to grant a licence to fight, they *demanded* a percentage of my fight fees for the defence of a title they didn't recognise which was being fought in a foreign country!

Who elected the people on the board? I'd like to know that and so would many others. We certainly didn't and we're the fighters, the men who make the money which gives the board members their status. We help to pay for them and have no say about their jobs. I felt they didn't do enough for Michael Watson. The BBBC is a self-governing body and I disagree with their rules. They're quick to take their percentage and slow to support you. We'd like to see more black guys there. I don't have confidence in some of the people on the board. There are a few who are all right, but there are others who shouldn't be in that position.

I don't think the public knows the powers they have. They can stop you fighting, they can demand payment from you and they can make you fight. It stinks to high heaven. I don't want to have anything to do with them any more. In my experience, they've shown more interest in the managers than in the boxers. It is people like me, successful boxers, who help to give them a good lifestyle and all I've had is hassle. It's a club for the boys.

They never liked Ambrose but, even so, he helped put British boxers on the map, which made them a lot more money. When I criticised them publicly for not granting Ambrose a manager's licence, they glibly responded that he hadn't applied, but nobody had the slightest doubt that, had Ambrose applied, he would unquestionably have been turned down.

In June, shortly before I returned to Miami to train for my contest with Barkley, I was invited to a lunch thrown in my honour at the Tower of London by my old regimental commanding officer, Colonel Patrick Shervington. Captain John O'Grady, my old team coach, was also there and I was deeply touched by their gesture.

Back in Miami, my dietitian, Randy Aaron, made me cut out red meat, butter and salt and encouraged turkey, pasta, fish and vegetable juices. My hand had healed and I was feeling super-fit again, ready to take on the world. Iran 'The Blade' Barkley was a serious opponent. He was a veteran who had won and lost the WBC title with Thomas Hearns and Roberto Duran. He was nicknamed 'The Blade' because he was from the Bronx in New York, the toughest neighbourhood in town, where gang members boasted about the people they had carved up and murdered. He was a junior member of the 'Black Spades' street gang. Barkley's manager, John Reetz, said if he stopped Iran fighting, the boxer would probably end up dead in a south Bronx gutter with a bullet through his head, or in jail.

He'd had a tough career, and the boxing journalist Harry Mullan put it in a nutshell:

> 'Barkley became the WBC champion with the luckiest punch of the year in 1988 when, bleeding from horrific slashes over both eyes and on the verge of a knockout defeat, he found one almighty right hand to flatten Hearns. But that was also the night his luck ran out. He needed around 70 stitches to repair his ravaged eyebrows, and when the wounds healed he set about spending the million dollars he had earned ... Benn has a powerful incentive to win impressively, as promoter Bob Arum plans to match him in a seven-figure pay-night with one of the division's major names like Duran, Nunn or even Sugar Ray Leonard. Beating Barkley will open the door, and should remove any lingering doubts that he is a middleweight of genuine world-class calibre. But it won't be easy, and the right hand which wrecked Thomas Hearns could well do the same to the explosive but sometimes vulnerable Dark Destroyer.'

Two days before my fight, Ambrose announced that the BBBC had sent him a letter saying that, as I had not paid the board the £2,500 fee for the De Witt fight, it would not give permission for me to fight Barkley. However, they would also expect another £7,300 from my purse of

$400,000 for the Barkley fight. God knows if this story was true, but at least it was what Ambrose told me. I told them that they would not get a penny from me because of their failure to recognise the title fights and also for having cost me over £1 million in refusing to let me fight Barkley and Roberto Duran in Britain.

People in Britain urged me to stay away from Iran Barkley. I had thought long and hard about our fight and decided it was a do or die situation. I was in two minds when I saw him. He was built like a brick shithouse. He was so ugly, tears wouldn't run down his face. Giving him the eye, however, I felt his bottle had gone and I would be the winner.

You can tell a man's fear from his eyes. I ran straight at him and my first punch separated his brain from his body. He looked like jelly. He was all over the place, wobbling and reeling. I was punching him, trying to nut him, elbow him, rough him up in every way possible. I beat the granny out of him, knocked him down, *boom*, up he got, *boom*, knocked him down again. I just gave it to him, left, right, left. I punched him until he went down on all fours and then I dug him one. Afterwards, I pole-axed him. Any minute now, I thought, we're going to have a riot. Americans can dish it out but they can't handle it when they're on the receiving end. I was ready to give it to him without a referee and without gloves.

I got Barkley on a technical knockout — he went down three times in the first round. It was a hell-for-leather fight, but I knew I had it in the bag from the weigh-in. But the scenes at the post-fight conference were a joke. When you're in the middle of a fight, you're all hyped up, the adrenalin's flowing. I don't remember doing it, but I saw on the TV afterwards that I'd hit him once when he was down. Barkley's camp made a right fuss, but they were just crying over spilt milk. The referee was one of the most experienced officials in the world, and even he said, 'It's the momentum, the eagerness. That happens sometimes in a fight.'

Barkley was going down from the beginning, anyway. What was important was that I had retained my WBO belt. On television afterwards, I ripped up my BBBC licence, saying, 'The Board have made it very hard for me, but they still want to get paid by the WBO. If they won't entertain me, then I won't entertain them.'

Bob Arum was ecstatic with my win. 'Nigel's undoubtedly the most exciting fighter in the world today and the best English boxer ever to come to the States,' he enthused. I returned triumphantly to London two days later on 20 August, asking to fight Sugar Ray Leonard, Tommy Hearns or Roberto Duran. My present to myself was a £90,000 Bentley. However, back in Britain, Chris Eubank, a man I really had no time for, was itching for a chance at my WBO middleweight title.

Barry Hearn, the promoter, claimed he was offering the highest purse ever to a British fighter and gave me a deadline to accept the Eubank challenge. Mendy was holding out for £1 million but I was keen to have a go at Eubank. Under the contract that was eventually signed, I received only £400,000, although the press reported that I received a million, and there was no option clause providing a re-match. Peter De Freitas told me that this is sometimes a standard clause and would have allowed me to have a second shot at Eubank within 90 days rather than waiting for three years, and that Mendy's lack of experience as a manager was the reason for not having it.

I thought I would have Eubank. I hated him. I remember thinking at the time that he needed to come down a couple of pegs and go away to America and win the world title and get some respect. My hatred towards him was not hype. I genuinely loathed him.

Eubank, in a rare moment of modesty, declared himself to be '... a boxer, slugger, trickster, craftsman, a mover, skillster and a chess player. Critics claim I am over-confident, but ability gives you that feeling. They say I'm arrogant. I say I'm assertive.' That may be acceptable but when he denigrated his own profession it wasn't only me who was angry with him. Fighting fans all over Britain were incensed when he called it 'a dirty business ... barbaric, a mug's game'. Eubank was from south London but had been brought up in the south Bronx, New York, since the age of 14. He said of me, 'Benn is a fraud, there is nothing genuine about the man ... he is not capable of teaching me any lessons ...'

Boxing has been very good to me and I don't like it when people knock the sport and say it's a mug's game and barbaric. When I first heard him say that, I thought the only mug was him, because boxing had made him a very wealthy man and given him a lifestyle he'd never have had. Before he began boxing, he was just like me, a kid from the street. I would never knock boxing. We don't need that kind of talk in the game. Boxing has already got a bad name after the Michael Watson incident and the last thing we need is more people putting it down.

You've got to stand very firm in boxing because it can be a very crooked game. You have to let people know that you are not going to be mugged and you won't let anybody take liberties with you, which happens in boxing all the time.

Towards the end of September 1990, I accepted the offer to fight Eubank and made peace with the British Boxing Board of Control. The Eubank fight was to be staged at the National Exhibition Centre in Birmingham on 18 November. A lot of pre-fight 'hate' between us was generated in the press but in my case, as I have already

said, it was 100 per cent genuine. The *Times* billed me as '...
a wild animal in the ring, and we had rarely, if ever, seen
anything like that in this country. He was the epitome of an
all-out warrior bringing a rage and fury into the ring that
one might only encounter in the United States. Only Mike
Tyson and Marvin Hagler have exuded such menace.'

Eubank was no newcomer to insults. He may have seen
the world through a rose-tinted monocle when he dressed
in his ridiculous clothes, but the garbage that flowed from
his mouth was closer to his real background.

Never a favourite of the BBBC, Mendy was making
further trouble as the fight neared. He insisted on being in
my corner, despite being banned by the board, and
threatened to sue over the issue in the High Court. A lot of
my money seemed to be spent on court battles. Mendy was
later fined £2,000 for appearing in my corner before the
fight. Earlier, he announced, 'This is a dangerous sport
made more dangerous by the board, who are a bunch of
buffoons and don't have a clue. They had said that under
no circumstances will I be able to go into Benn's corner. The
only way I won't be there is if I'm six feet under! It's
becoming more than boxing now — it's a war between me
and the board.'

The NEC was packed and our fight attracted the
biggest celebrity turnout for a sporting event the country
had seen. More than 150 stars turned up.

Losing my title to Eubank was gutting, but looking
back he beat me fair and square, and I boxed well, too. I
was practically blind in one eye for most of the match, and I
pushed Eubank like he'd never been pushed before. I
fought till I had nothing left to offer, and the ref called it a
day after about three minutes of the ninth of twelve
scheduled rounds.

Eubank became more respectful towards me after the
fight but I was gutted. Chris had damaged my eye and

broken my heart. I wanted a re-match as soon as possible. Eubank said of me, 'He hit me in the guts, the mouth and on my head — man, it hurt. I didn't know people had that kind of power. I had to keep asking the Lord to help me out on this one. That man hits mega, mega hard. He is one in a million — I didn't know people could have that kind of power. He was strong enough to kill me. His power is savage and he extended me the way nobody else in life has done. For that, I love the man.'

The referee said of our fight, 'I've refereed 79 world title fights and this was in the very top category. It was too bad one had to lose. They are both champions in my book, but I was doing my duty to stop it, so Benn can come back and win that title again. Benn was really gallant, but just could not see out of the left eye.'

I had two goals now. To beat Eubank and win another world title. But first I had to pick myself up again and shake off the disappointment of this fight. And so I turned to my family.

15

WEDDING NIGHT BLUES

After Eubank beat me, I thought there was no better way of shooting myself than getting married. Sharron was there for me when I went down to Watson and she was there for me again after Eubank. In spite of our somewhat unpredictable relationship, there was deep love. I asked her to marry me on my birthday, giving us two months to prepare.

We'd already been engaged for a couple of years without naming the day. I might have been in a zimmer frame by the time I'd got around to marriage had I not been encouraged to set a date. The engagement itself had caught her totally off-guard. I had asked her to become my fiancée at a New Year's Eve party and slipped a huge diamond ring on her finger. Then I got down on one knee in front of my parents and proposed to her. She was so shocked that she spilled her drink but said yes. I would have laid her out if it had been otherwise! Not really, but then it was the third happiest day of my life. The other two were when our children were born.

For the first time in years, we had some space to ourselves. My next fight was some months away and I planned a romantic wedding in Las Vegas.

First stop on our journey into wedlock was Bell Harbor,

Miami, to kit us out with some wicked outfits. I bought most of Sharron's clothes. She and I have always had similar tastes in fashion. Her wedding dress was unbelievable. She looked like a princess. I had on a black number and she wore white. Her outfit cost about £6,000. It was really expensive and I feel like taking it back because she hasn't worn it. I fell in love with the outfit and it made me love her even more. It was like an evening dress and she looked stunning in it. I had wanted a wedding in England but that would have cost £100,000 and involved too many people. We preferred a small ceremony.

Sharron's brother Scottie, her sister Joanne, Ambrose Mendy, Bob Arum (my USA promoter) and his girlfriend and other American friends came to the wedding. I was really nervous and the night before our nuptials we slept apart. We had chosen the Little White Chapel where Joan Collins had got married and, afterwards, a reception at Caesar's Palace Hotel where they had specially opened the roof for us. The wedding party stayed at the Alexis Hotel. Sharron and I had a beautiful suite with a jacuzzi the size of a swimming pool, a massive double bed and huge bouquets of flowers in every room.

When she walked into the chapel to marry me, she looked stunning. I tried not to look at her but she kept her eyes on me. I nervously rubbed my hands together. The ceremony was beautiful. We exchanged vows and kissed tenderly.

Ambrose made a speech at the party at Caesar's Palace but it was hard to follow. I thanked everybody for coming and then it was time to cut the cake and drink champagne. Sharron drank a little too much — in fact, so much that she became steadily more drunk and any romantic notions I entertained for our bridal suite went out of the window. She was out like a light. I sat up watching telly. I asked if a kiss might be out of question but felt there was a possibility she might throw up. I wished I'd brought a blow-up rubber doll; I might have got a better response from that than my bride. What a way to spend your wedding night!

The next day, the first of our married life, we started to argue and continued doing so all the way back to England. What a disappointment. I had placed romantic messages behind the bed and wanted our time there to be really special. I fantasised that it would be the happiest day of our lives. As we were leaving for the airport, we argued again and Sharron walked off, leaving the wedding cake and her bags. I had to go back and get them. Then we argued for the first four hours on the plane back home and, for a further eight hours, refused to speak to one another. So this was wedded bliss!

On our return, I had to get down to training for my fight against Robbie Sims at Bethnal Green on 3 April. If I lost this one I'd be washed up for good. Sims had never been stopped in an 11-year career and was the half-brother of my idol, Marvin Hagler.

Around this time, I was also becoming disillusioned with Mendy. We began drifting apart. And I started questioning the fact that I was doing all the hard work — fighting and training — and Ambrose was the one with the big house and swimming pool. This wasn't quite right as far as I was concerned. Nevertheless, he was still making arrangements for the Sims fight which was originally planned for the NEC until death threats were made against me.

They were telephoned to Mendy's offices and referred to my military connections with the Royal Regiment of Fusiliers, who advised me to take them seriously, particularly as I had been in Northern Ireland. I had always been conscious of this type of thing and made sure I was even more careful regarding my movements and cars. At the end of the day, however, I had to accept that the IRA, if indeed it was them making the threats and not Ambrose trying to sell more tickets, would always get you if that's what they really wanted. I had no personal quarrel with them.

Before fighting Sims, I had a ridiculous offer to fight Chris Eubank for £250,000 and rejected it out of hand. Eubank then rejected my demands for the purse to be split down the middle and said I had priced myself out of the market and that his next objective was a fight with Michael Watson.

On my return from training for six weeks in Miami, I felt a little nervous but was, nevertheless, confident that I would beat Sims. I would be more controlled in my next fight. Although Marvin was my hero, Sims bad-mouthed me before the fight. He called me a monster, a 'junkyard dog' who didn't care about anyone else and said of himself, 'I've never been stopped and I've never been dropped on the floor and I've not come all this way to take a fall for the first time.' I'd heard it all before.

Robbie Sims was a very good fighter. He'd been around a long time and was a good warhorse. He was a southpaw and I was wary of fighting him. At the time I still had Vic Andreeti as my trainer but things were starting to change. Peter De Freitas was now working with me and it was vital I regained a strong position. My army discipline helped me focus my energies. After the Eubank fight, this was going straight back into the deep end. It would have been the end of my career if I'd lost. You can only drop so much. Sims was not a journeyman like you get in England.

I came in strong from the start, jabbing him in the face, giving it to him in the body. He was underweight so I knew he had prepared for the fight but I had reserves of power to call on if needed. Sims was stronger than anyone I've ever met, including Watson and Eubank, and I had to watch out for his body punching.

At first, I was a little worried that I'd chosen to fight him but then that helped my mental resolve to beat him. In the past, I've tended to be over-confident as well as immature against certain opponents.

My left hook exploded on his chin in the seventh round and knocked him spark out. The ref stopped the fight a couple of minutes into the round and I thought, *Yes*, I'm back!

After the fight, Marvin Hagler (meeting him was like meeting God) came to me and praised my style. 'You gave him a fucking good hiding. You was good. You was good,' he told me. Then he pulled Sims aside and told him, 'Handle defeat gracefully. Respect the guy, he beat you and that's it.'

The following week, Mendy was due to appear in court on the £65,000 fraud conspiracy for which he was sent to prison. I gave character evidence on his behalf and later visited him inside and paid about £15,000 for his court case. I had also lent him my Porsche which he smashed up. It cost me £6,000 in repairs. I then paid further lawyers' fees but no money was paid back. I would have stuck by Ambrose 100 per cent but, after a while, I thought this was no longer a wise thing to do. I'd lost a lot of money and I had lent him another £2,000 in prison. It was time to say ta-ta. But it was difficult severing a loyalty that had been so absolute for several years.

My next fight, against Kid Milo (his real name is Winston Walters), who was then reigning WBC International super-middle king, at Brentwood on 3 July, proved to be another turning point for me. Following the fight, Vic Andreeti and I called it a day and, after our amicable parting, I trained with Graham Moughton at Barry Hearn's Matchroom gym in Romford. Milo had lost to Eubank a year earlier, but only after the eighth round, with a stoppage on cuts. I dispatched him in the fourth. I hit him so hard he could hardly get back on his feet.

I was back on course to challenge Eubank until the tragic fight on Saturday, 21 September 1991 when Watson suffered brain damage in his title contest against Eubank. Watson was winning the fight until the eleventh round, when Eubank put him on the ropes with a crushing uppercut. Nobody was to know at the time how seriously he'd been injured. I was ringside and thought it was right that the referee, Roy Francis, allowed the fight to go on. Michael would have beaten Eubank. I visited him in hospital a few days later and tried to talk to him and comfort his girlfriend. It hurt to see him in that condition.

In October, I announced that Mendy and I no longer had anything to do with each other and that I would not be taking part in over-the-top activities which had been the Ambrose trademark of the past. It had been good while it lasted and at least it was another learning experience.

For my next fight, against Lenzie Morgan at Brentwood on 26 October, I moved up in weight from middle to super-middle. Eubank had also moved up and I still had him very much in my sights. I knew that Morgan would be a tough cookie and that it wasn't going to be an easy fight because I'd seen him in the States. But I knew I had the power and was determined to beat him. It was a good test for me. It put me under a lot of pressure which I liked and I was pleased with the result, winning on points against a difficult opponent.

A few days after the fight, I spent a little time with Geoffrey Dickens, the Tory MP, filming a campaigning pop video for the anti-child abuse rap record 'It's OK to say No'. It warned youngsters to stay away from strangers and featured Mr Dickens and me chanting the lyrics. I was to become involved in music in a much bigger way later on, but for the moment I had to go straight back into my training routine for the next bout, against Hector Lescano at the G-Mex Centre in Manchester on 7 December.

Hector's nickname was 'The Dog' but, as one journalist said, 'He didn't come to lie down ...' He hit the floor in the third, though.

After the fight, I was challenged by his manager Mickey Duff to a £150,000 showdown with Henry Wharton who offered to share the purse on a 50-50 split. Duff said his man was the most exciting puncher in Britain. 'We will put big money to Benn if he thinks he can handle Wharton's fierce punching.'

I waited a couple of years before proving them wrong. In the meantime, Barry Hearn began talks for a re-match with Eubank, saying we could gross £2 million. First, however, he wanted me to fight Canadian Dan Sherry at Muswell Hill on 19 February.

Sherry, a Canadian, came close to beating Eubank in Brighton in 1991 but lost the WBO challenge after he was head-butted in the tenth round. Hearn said, 'Sherry has given me aggro since he lost to Chris Eubank and I want Nigel to cork him once and for all.'

Both Sherry and his cornerman Pepe Correa tried to give me aggro at a pre-fight press conference. Both said I would end the fight lying on the canvas. 'We're here to whip you.' When they began haranguing me, I walked off. I wasn't going to get involved with the loser. The ref stopped the fight in the third.

Chris Eubank, with whom I had been itching for a re-match, kept avoiding my challenge. The WBO recognised me as the number one contender and I felt that Eubank was just a piece of chicken shit to put off the fight. How could he call himself a world champion and be scared to come in the ring with me? I had never turned down other fighters. I was quite prepared to face Iran Barkley again even though he swore he'd kill me in revenge for my earlier victory. But Eubank wouldn't face me. When he was warned that he would forfeit his title if he did not go through with the mandatory defence, all Eubank would say was that people couldn't tell him what to do. 'The only thing I have to do is stay black and die,' was his smart-ass comment. He called himself 'Simply the Best', but I reckoned he was 'Simply a Pest'.

Dad says my fight with Sugarboy Malinga was one of my worst performances so I can't argue about that. He told me afterwards, 'You won it and just thank your lucky stars you had the decision. If it had been my decision, the best you would have got was a draw. But it was one of your off-days and any fighter can have an off-day so don't worry about it.' Point taken, Dad! But the judges gave it to me on points, anyway.

Although negotiations seemed to have reached a stalemate with Eubank, he suddenly relented and agreed to a re-match in September. In the meantime, my challenge to Italian Mauro Galvano had finally paid dividends and he agreed to defend his WBC super-middleweight title against me in Marino, Italy on 3 October. As a result, the WBO were forced to drop me from their ratings. My long-term plan was postponed. I would meet Eubank the following year, 1993. With the Mauro fight scheduled, my chance had finally come for a shot at a second world title championship.

16

WBC
SUPER-MIDDLEWEIGHT
CHAMPION

I wanted to change trainers for my WBC super-middleweight title fight against Mauro Galvano and Jimmy Tibbs fitted the bill perfectly. He had trained world champions Lloyd Honeyghan, Jim Watt and Charlie Magri. Michael Watson had also trained with him and Jimmy was in his corner during his tragic last fight against Eubank.

Jimmy is one of the best trainers around. He had a promising professional boxing career himself until he got into a bit of bother in the early Seventies. Things got a little wild with enemies of his family who were very well known and lived in the East End. Jimmy tried to take the law into his own hands and, unfortunately, by doing so, cut short his career.

Just before he was sent to prison, he'd been hailed as the 'golden boy' of British boxing. He had wanted to avenge wrongs done to his family. Someone had tried to blow up a car containing Jimmy and his young son, and there had been other attacks as well. Since that time, Jimmy has reformed. Now he is a born-again Christian, just like my dad, and the pair of them get on very well.

I began training for my fights in Tenerife. Going there removed the distractions of London and the domestic conflicts which arise in most relationships and which can lead to debilitating emotional upsets. Training is such an intense activity that it is almost impossible to do with a family around you. The Canary Islands also offered a more temperate climate in winter and the opportunity for high-altitude running on Mount Teide.

There is nothing more beautiful and fulfilling than running at an altitude of about 8,000 feet among snow-capped peaks in bright sunshine, well above the clouds. I can retreat into a world of my own, my own galaxy. Just me and my music and, later, the satisfaction that comes from physically punishing yourself. You can clear your mind of all anxieties and problems in that surrealistic 'moonscape' where they shot *Planet of the Apes*, and be at peace with the world. That's where I get my 'high'. When I was training for the Wharton fight, Sean, my cook, used to accompany me, driving behind me as I ran past each milepost. I'd run six to eight miles and then increase it to ten and even more. That's equivalent to running up to 15 miles at sea level. At other times, my father would come with me and drive the car, as would Peter De Freitas.

Back at my beach-front apartment in Torviscas, there was a gym and boxing ring where Jimmy trained me. He was particularly good with the pads and took a hell of a slamming from me every day, brainwashing me with his technique while I hammered away at him. Both Jim and Peter then joined me in the gym, often working out themselves. I listened to their advice, but at the end of the day, they knew that *I* am the boss. It's not what they said that matters, it's what *I* said. I know what my body can do and how much I should train. If I wanted time off I'd take it without any feelings of guilt afterwards. If I wanted to go to a nightclub and stay out most of the night during my six-week training period, I'd do so. That was my prerogative.

Jimmy Tibbs set up a training schedule — this is it straight from the horse's mouth: 'We're going to start with loosening up and stretching exercises, then do three or four rounds' shadow boxing with weights on the hands and one round with them off, then four or five more with pads. After that, we'll do some more shadow boxing, skipping and ground work and have a good loosening up.

'Weight training will take place every other day and then, for two weeks before the fight, we'll have a sparring partner for nine to ten rounds per day. We may take it down to six some days. The art of the game is to peak on the night. I don't worry about an off-day here or there. Just relax and come back again. Nigel's a mature professional now who can go the distance. He's a very solid puncher and is physically strong.

'But it doesn't matter how strong you are, everyone gets tired, even if you've been training for months. A good fighter has got to get through that. He's matured and grown up and knows how to pace himself and when to let go. He's a mature professional now. His main strength is his punch but he's also got smarter. Rather than bang, bang, bang, he ducks and dives and makes a man miss. He can't keep on taking whacks all the time.

'He's intelligent enough to listen as well. Some people won't be shown things but Nigel asks and, even more importantly, listens when you give him advice. Nigel is a very determined person. If he can get that tunnel vision, that is how I want him. I also like him as a person. He's got a good heart and he is a very gentle soul really. I know his family and his dad and I can see where they come from and I like what I see. They're a very honest family. When we train in Tenerife, Nigel is very popular with the public. He takes time out for everyone, old grannies and young kids, and sits down with them after training to sign autographs and chat to them. His dad, Dickson, is also very popular.

Everyone keeps asking after him. I know Nigel was very kind to one of his disabled fans, Timmy Matheson, who is a paraplegic. Timmy met Nigel at a charity do and Nigel spotted him and invited him to sit with his mates at a ringside table. He now makes sure he always gets a ringside seat at his British venues.'

Timmy Matheson is a great kid. He's got cerebral palsy, and I first came across him at a boxing dinner ten or eleven years ago. I saw him with his mum at the back in a corner, and no one was really paying much attention to them. Some people were even walking away from them, and it really got to me badly because nobody seemed to care about them.

I told the organisers that unless he sat next to me on the top table, I was walking out there and then. They brought him over and we have been great friends ever since. He can't speak, but his eyes say everything. I look into them and know he understands every word I say. When I ran the London Marathon, I did it for cerebral palsy and for Timmy.

A lot of people make arbitrary judgements about what you should or shouldn't do. That's not me. I don't want to die a boring man. I live for every minute. I had several friends who owned clubs and discos in Las Americas and they let me use them during the day to mix music and then invited me to dee-jay in the evening. Apart from being on top of Mount Teide, nothing gives me more pleasure, or is more relaxing, than dee-jaying or working on my own mixes. Sean, my cook and friend, was also a DJ and we did quite a bit of clubbing before the Henry Wharton fight. I had to smile when the press tried to make a feature out of the fact that I had brought my children down to Tenerife for a weekend shortly before defending my title. They said such a distraction could lose me the fight. Win it, more likely! It made me play happy families and kept me inside the flat.

To ensure that I had no other distractions, my girlfriend at the time gave me a present before I left London — a full-size, blow-up rubber doll! She has a good sense of humour and I can reveal that the doll remained folded up in my bottom drawer throughout my stay, although I did offer her to a friend who turned her down, saying he preferred blondes.

I trained very hard for the Galvano fight. The WBC belt was superior to the WBO super-middleweight title and was recognised by all boxing authorities worldwide. I aimed to bring it back from Italy. I was confident of success although I distrusted the Italians and feared they would get up to dirty tricks in trying to retain it. When Jimmy was in Italy with Lloyd Honeyghan, he knocked out Gianfranco Rosi for a European title but the story on the street was that the referee took nearly half a minute to count to ten and only signalled the fight as over when he realised Rosi wouldn't get up for a week. They also seemed to mess Pat Clinton around when he beat Salvatore Fanni by giving him weight scales which showed he was 2lb over and he took the weight off only to find he was 2lb under at the offical weigh-in.

Winning the title would put me back on course for large purses and bring me closer to retirement. A boxer can only go on for a limited time when he puts his body through a punishing regime as often as I had. Beating Galvano would also create a record in that I would be the only boxer this century to win two world titles outside Britain. Up until that time I had had 35 fights, 33 wins (29 inside the distance) and two defeats.

I would have travelled to Timbuctu if it meant winning a belt, so Italy was quite convenient, even though I hated fighting there. Galvano was an OK bloke, but the crowd was really hostile — they couldn't take the fact that a black guy was trying for the title, and they started spitting at me, and pelting me with coins. It was just a racist thing. In England, you don't get that — nobody really cares if you're black or white, as long as you give them a good show. In Italy, it was totally different.

But it took more than a few jeers to put me off what I had come there to do. I was ready for Galvano big time, and really gave it to him. He got battered left, right and centre. But even after I'd clearly beaten him, the Italians tried to take my victory away from me.

In the second round, I connected with a good, powerful right-hander which split Galvano's eye. It was obvious he wasn't going to be able to last much longer. Now, the WBC rules state that if a fight ends inside three rounds because of a foul, the match is declared a technical draw. Galvano's camp saw the mess he was in and tried to pull him out before the fourth, claiming that I had head-butted him to cause the eye injury. It was just a load of bullshit, of course — I'd punched him fairly and squarely — and the Italians had no leg to stand on, but it pissed me off because it could have cost me the title.

Fortunately, the ref saw sense, and Galvano's third-round retirement gave me the match. I was almost ready to cry. I thrust my arms in the air and shouted, 'YES! YES! BENN IS BACK!' The Italians didn't like that much, but hey, I was now the WBC Super-Middleweight Champion, two-time champion of the world. I had plenty to celebrate. Chris Eubank had been ringside, and at one stage I remember leaning over to him through the ropes and saying, 'Now we can do business.' He nodded and said he was ready ...

I returned to Britain as champion, but for some reason it didn't really seem as if I'd won a world title. I suppose it was because of the way they treated me, and I really took it out on Nicky Piper in London for my next fight.

Nicky was said to be a near-genius. When we fought at Muswell Hill on 12 December, he entered the ring with an IQ of 153. Let me tell you, when he left it was more like an IQ of 1. He was a big guy — 6ft 3in — and when he stripped down, I had to admire the shape he was in. His muscles were showing much better than mine, and he really looked like he'd been doing his training.

Nicky came from Frank Warren's stable, so I now had my first dealings with Frank since we'd had those problems a few years back. But we were polite enough to each other, and showed each other the proper respect.

As I said, Piper was a tall guy, and I wondered how I was going to get hold of his jaw. I've also got to say he was a strong fucker, and seemed to be able to absorb some heavy punches in that big old head of his. And he managed to hurt me, too, until I got the measure of him. In the eleventh round I delivered a blistering succession of punches to Piper's head which sent him reeling. Jimmy Tibbs said to me afterwards that he had said a silent prayer when I laid into Piper's head. He didn't want a repetition of what had happened to Michael Watson and couldn't wait for the ref to stop the fight. He'd had a terrible flashback.

Finally, the ref decided he'd seen enough. I was declared the winner on a technical knockout.

Now that I had secured my superior belt, Eubank was fuming. He didn't like the fact that I held the premier belt and could dictate the terms of our next fight. I told everybody that perhaps I should be like him and line up ten fighters and fight a bum a month. But that wasn't my style. I'd fight anyone, and not pick and choose like Eubank.

On 6 March 1993, I retained my world title in Glasgow against Mauro Galvano. It was a long 12 rounds, but I won on points even though he caught me with a good shot at the end which made my legs go.

My next fight was against Lou Gent, the Cockney WBC International Champion, at Olympia on 26 June. This was a fight that whetted the public's appetite for the match everybody was waiting for — the unification fight against Eubank which was scheduled for 9 October in Manchester.

I had total respect for Lou Gent. We didn't go in for any of the pre-fight stuff, slagging each other off. But, as I've said before, you can tell a lot from a man's eyes, and when I studied his I could tell that he was totally intimidated by me. He went down three times in the third and twice in the fourth, but respect to him, because he kept coming back. But he was weak by the end, and the ref had to give it to me in the fourth.

So the next fight was the big one against Eubank. But before that, something even more important happened. On 12 July 1993, Sharron gave birth to my second daughter, Renée — the most beautiful little girl in the world. I didn't even know that Sharron was pregnant until she told me in the middle of an argument.

We were quarrelling, and I told her she was overweight. 'Look at the state of you,' I said.

She turned on me. 'You *bastard*! I'm pregnant.'

In sheer surprise and shock, I stupidly retorted, 'Who's the father?' before realising my inexcusable mistake. I was, of course. She went mad, but I didn't mean it to come out like that.

Sharron had a difficult time with the pregnancy, but the result was wonderful, although Renée got us really worried when she went blue at birth, and had to have a tube inserted up her nose. I thought she was going to die, and felt so angry and helpless I could have punched someone. She has big, big eyes and a cute face. Such a beautiful little girl, and funny with it. Really bright and inquisitive. At six months she had already worked out the TV controls.

I was the first British boxer to be paid a purse of £1 million for a British-staged fight. My opponent, Eubank, who held a lesser title, had to accept £850,000. A global TV audience of over 100 million was expected. Our measurements, apart from Eubank's swollen head, were very similar. We were evenly matched in height, weight, reach and chest. The bout was staged at Manchester United's Old Trafford Stadium because neither Eubank nor I wanted to meet at Tottenham's White Hart Lane as that is where Michael had suffered brain damage.

Peter De Freitas rubbed salt into Eubank's wounded pride by saying, 'We now have a contract with Barry Hearn and Don King, who acts for Showtime TV in America. We are being paid £1 million but I understand Eubank is on considerably less. This is because Nigel Benn is recognised as the premier champion. King and TV are only interested in our WBC super-middleweight title. They want the winner in unification bouts with James Toney and Michael Nunn. Eubank's WBO championship is not really relevant. It hasn't the prestige of the big three — the WBC, WBA and IBF. Now, it is finally settled that Nigel goes into the ring as champion. Chris will have to wait for him on the night. The fight will be handled by WBC officials and Nigel has all the rights of the title holder — as well as the major purse.'

Eubank's explosive mouth would now be publicly put to the test and, to help him remember, the newspapers printed some of his big-headed remarks which he was forced to swallow after the contest. He had said of me, 'I want to put Benn on the floor — just 10 or 11 seconds will do. Long enough to leave no room for controversy ... He said we can now meet for the re-match

— even my wife thinks he will duck it ... I'm a clever, intelligent boxer, but he is an ignorant man ... Benn is a Fairy Liquid fighter and one day the bubble will burst. Class will always prevail — I have it, he doesn't.'

At the press conference, I started as I meant to go on. I walked round to his chair and snapped, 'I don't fucking like you!' It's true — I really thought he was a total prick, with his monocle and stupid clothes, pretending he was from the silver spoon society. He still talks a load of bollocks to this day!

Forty-seven thousand people were at Old Trafford for what was going to be one of the biggest fights in British history. The atmosphere was absolutely brilliant — Old Trafford was the best venue I have ever fought in. It was the only time I ever had a £1 million purse, but to be honest, I was still reeling from being world champion. The money was nice, but it was only secondary.

It was a long fight — the full 12 rounds, but by the end I was sure the match was mine. And I wasn't alone — when a draw was announced, the crowd booed, and the boxing press afterwards seemed to be on my side.

I was disgusted with the score. I was convinced I had won and believed, like many others, that I had beaten Eubank on points, even with the lost penalty point. Hearn wasn't looking too happy with his man so he obviously feared the worst. I was too angry to face the press conference. Judge Castellano had me winning in the last six rounds, but what the hell was I doing in the first six? Later, yielding to pressure, they released details of the judges' scorecards, which makes it clear that new rules ought to be drawn up on the scoring system. Harry Gibbs scored a victory for Eubank; Carol Castellano and Chuck Hassert scored a points victory for me, before deduction of the penalty point. This is the official score:

OFFICIAL SCORECARDS
[My scores are recorded first]

	GIBBS	CASTELLANO	HASSETT
R1	9-10	9-10	9-10
R2	9-10	9-10	10-9
R3	10-9	9-10	9-10
R4	10-9	10-9	10-9
R5	9-10	9-10	10-10
R6	10-10	9-10	9-10
R7	10-9	10-9	9-10
R8	9-10	10-9	10-9
R9	9-10	10-9	10-9
R10	10-9	10-9	10-9
R11	9-10	10-9	9-10
R12	10-9	10-9	10-9

Totals: 114-115 (Eubank)   115-113 (Benn)   115-114 (Benn)

I was then deducted a point by each judge for a low blow in the sixth:

Totals: 113-115 (Eubank) 114-113 (Benn) 114-114 (Benn)

Don King, the American promoter, had taken part in the promotion of this match and guaranteed the purse. Under the terms of our contract, both Eubank and I, regardless of whether we won or lost, would have had to sign with Don King for each of our next three fights, and King was, at that time, negotiating with Frank Warren for a TV tie-up in the future. In our respective agreements, no option was given for the unlikely event of a draw, as a result of which Eubank was no longer committed to King. That was good news for Hearn. He had already lost Chris Pyatt to Frank

Warren and would not have wanted to lose one of his big earners to King. Eubank was worth in the region of £200,000 per fight to him, so God was obviously smiling on the pair that evening.

My only consolation after the fight was being able to forget some of my anger through the diversion of a superb party laid on by my pal Rolex Ray. He'd organised a Manchester club for an all-night bash and then hired a Pullman coach at £2,000 a day — the only one in Britain and which had been used by Madonna — for our return to London the following day.

17

GERALD McCLELLAN

American promoter Don King is a larger-than-life figure, and a powerful man. I signed a three-fight deal with him in October 1993, the first of which would be my mandatory defence against Henry Wharton in four months' time. King joined forces with Frank Warren, with the hope that Jarvis Astaire and Mickey Duff would participate in the future. He described me as 'an awesome performer. The Americans will love his style.'

Don himself is not short of style. He came over to Britain for my fight and wore his diamond-and-gold jewellery at a press conference in the House of Commons. Opinions vary about Don. Some wouldn't touch him with a barge pole; others have made mega bucks. Larry Holmes, who was a heavyweight champion, said, 'Even now, people whisper in my ear about how he exploited me all those years. Well, I made 20 million bucks with Don King. If that's exploitation, keep it coming.'

Another American heavyweight, Randall 'Tex' Cobb, said of Don, 'Don King is one of the great humanitarians of our time. He has risen above prejudice. He has screwed everybody he has ever been around — hog, dog or frog, it don't matter to Don. If you got a quarter, he wants the first 26 cents.'

He's a tough man. He spent time in prison for manslaughter after growing up in a Cleveland ghetto. Now he's worth around half a billion dollars and has a lot of clout. People don't mess with Don.

I trained in Tenerife for the fight — described as the 'finest' in my career — the title bout with Henry Wharton. Sean, my cook, Jimmy Tibbs, my trainer, and Peter De Freitas, my personal manager, accompanied me.

Apart from being a good companion and friend, Sean is a terrific cook who always ensured that I took my vitamin pills. I once met a chap called Arthur who wrote about nutrition and on reading his theories, I was convinced this man would make me a world champion. I flew to his home town in America to check it out and he drew up a list of vitamins for me to take, as well as a nutrition plan. He suggested plenty of iron tablets — about 50 a day, which supplies more oxygen to the blood. The diet included eating chicken and fish for breakfast. Sean would cook me salmon, which I love with sweet potatoes, vegetables and red peppers. In total, I had to take about 120 tablets a day to ensure I was getting the right amount of vitamins and minerals, such as calcium and potassium.

I needed all of these supplements throughout my rigorous training schedule, otherwise my body would seize up. I could lose up to six pounds of body fluid in one training session and I wanted to come out firing on all cylinders and give it my best shot. Training for this fight was hard. It really brought home to me the strain I was putting my body through. That was an indication I should think about quitting.

I got my schedule down to a fine art. I'd get up about 9.00am and have breakfast of fish or chicken and a bowl of porridge with a banana. Then I'd take 15 iron tablets, two zinc, two multivitamin and some other tablets and, afterwards, drive to Mount Teide to a level of 8,000–9,000ft above sea level. That would take 45 minutes, by which time the tablets would have been digested. The air up there is really thin. It took me quite a long time to understand about altitude training but I eventually mastered it.

I ran about eight miles every day for a week. Then I increased the distance to ten and then twelve, before reducing it to eight, and then up again to as high as fifteen. I was careful not to overdo it. As I've said, I love the altitude; it's the only place where I feel so much at peace with myself. There is no one to bother you. It's like paradise. It's so beautiful.

For lunch, Sean would vary my diet. One day it might be tropical fruits, or chicken and pasta or fish. I had fish three or four times a week. Fish, chicken and pasta, in rotation. I'm not a fussy eater. I can eat anything except mushrooms and butter beans.

After my training session, which included gym work with Jimmy as I've already described, I'd relax in front of the television or play Playstation games. The body needs time to relax. We used to train three times a day but that was too excessive, so we cut it down to twice a day. Jimmy knew how to get me buzzing. He and I both liked the pads and he always got the best out of me. He is very aggressive but knows what he is doing. Some people who had trained me in the past didn't really know what they were doing. Jimmy pushes me to my limit, which is important. We tried to cover every muscle of the body, even the neck. We put 100 per cent effort into training.

The training is so intense that it is difficult to believe you're putting yourself through such a strenuous regime. Compared to that, the fight is easy. Timing is also very important. You've got to pace yourself and not peak too early. You have to know when to slow down or even stop for a day. I'm not going to kill myself. I only wish I knew what I know now when I was 25.

Another thing I learned was not to underestimate my opponent. Henry is a very good fighter and he reminds me of myself. He had knocked out almost everybody else, just like I had, but I thought he still had a lot to learn and I would start teaching him. He was a dangerous fighter, but I'd been with them all — Barkley, De Witt, Simms, Watson, Eubank. I'd been with all the tough guys and I wasn't scared. I just wanted to be the king of the tough guys.

Wharton was one of my toughest fights. Not necessarily the hardest, but certainly the toughest. Although I beat him on points and retained my title, I'd never come out of a ring as bruised as I did after that fight. My kidneys were quite badly affected and I had to undergo hospital checks which, thankfully, quelled my fears and found my kidneys to be 100 per cent OK. I'd been whacked in the kidneys before, but I'd never felt it like I did with Wharton. I thought our fight would run the whole course so I didn't go for a knockout. Henry could be a future world champion. He was a strong boy.

I think the incentive for me to prove myself in that fight was less for me, which was also a sign of getting older. I wasn't as hungry. Immediately after the bout, I felt I was losing it a bit because this was the worst I'd ever been beaten up, worse than with Eubank. I needed a new challenge, a new title to keep the hunger alive. I think if I had been the contender, I would have sparked him, but I was the veteran now, the old boy. Let him go for it. Everyone thought it was my best fight but I wasn't sure.

A couple of days later I fell over on the stairs outside my flat. I was in lots of pain and went back to hospital. It was as though there was a voice telling me, 'Hey, hurry up and end your career.' Still, Wharton fought well, but not well enough.

In spite of my pain, I still went out afterwards to a champagne party Ray threw in a Kensington disco, and dee-jayed until the early hours of the morning. Booze was flowing by the gallon but I was too absorbed as a DJ to drink much. Besides, my kidneys were aching. The next day, I passed blood and went immediately to hospital at Redbridge — on the same site I had once guarded as a security man.

Wharton also said it was the toughest fight of his career and was grateful I had given him the opportunity.

Throughout this time, my personal life was as traumatic as ever. Things had been going badly with Sharron, and we just seemed to spend our time hurting each other and arguing. We split up in a whirlwind of acrimony, although it was not until 1996 that we actually divorced. When I think back on my life with Sharron, I feel bitter. OK, I know I did things wrong, but it takes two to tango, and no one can claim that she can't also take some share of the blame.

By this time, though, I was together with Carolyne, the beautiful woman I was later to marry. Over the years, we've been through some tough times. But she's always been there for me.

We first got to know each other in about 1991, and when we first met, I knew from the way she made me feel that she was different. Even in the early days, if we couldn't see each other, we'd speak on the phone for hours on end, talking about anything that came into our heads. She was not like the other girls I had known — she was particularly genuine and intelligent. She understood me for what I am, and I, in turn, felt an affinity with her like I'd never felt before. She was, and is, everything to me.

Carolyne never asked me for anything, unlike some of the other gold-diggers out there I'd met from time to time. She brought a whole new meaning to my life, and I will always be grateful to her for being there for me, for understanding the pressure I was under and sticking by me through thick and thin. I know I've done things to hurt her in the past, but since meeting her I have changed so much for the better — I'm a different man, and it's all thanks to

Carolyne. She is now my wife, my lover, my mentor and my very, very best friend.

It was more than six months until my next fight. At the beginning of my career, I was fighting 13 times a year. Now I knew the end was in sight, so I started becoming more selective, concentrating on the big-money fights. Juan Giminez came and went on 10 September 1994, beaten on points, and then there was a five-month build-up until I went into the ring with Gerald McClellan.

Carolyne and I had moved out to LA earlier on in 1994, because we needed to get away from the pressure of being in England. And in LA we had some wild times. The first day we arrived, we checked into a fantastic hotel, and it was like paradise — we were on our own, no one to hassle me, money rolling in. But we couldn't live in hotels all the time, so I found us a wicked apartment in the Marina del Ray. It took me a week to furnish it to my taste, with floor-to-ceiling TVs, a huge seven-foot bed, sofas, the works.

I bought my Porsche 959 out in LA, too. I wandered into a showroom and said to the guy, 'How much is this Porsche 959?' He told me it was such-and-such thousand dollars.

'I want that Porsche,' I told him.

'OK,' he said. He walked off and didn't return. He must have thought I was one of those rough street hoodlums or something.

So two days later, I had a banker's draft ready. I went back to the showroom and said to the guy, 'You thought I couldn't buy this car, didn't you?'

He spluttered, 'No, sir ... no, sir.'

'Yes, you did.' I just thought, Fuck you, I've got the money. I assumed he was just looking at me thinking, He's a black man, he can't have all that. Well, like fuck I can't, mate.

So now I looked the part — wicked apartment, flash car. On one occasion, I was driving it along the marina, and this police car pulled up beside me. The cop inside called out 'Hey, you're the boxer, right?' We were doing about 5 mph as he drove alongside me, and carried on chatting. In the meantime, a huge queue of traffic is building up, all crawling along behind us. The cop didn't give a shit.

They were like that, the cops in LA. I was once caught doing 120 mph on the way to San Francisco, when I was stopped by the police. But instead of booking me, the guy asked for an autograph for his son! My face was beginning to be recognised around the place. On one occasion, I was sitting in a café when this cop comes up to me and asks for my number and suggests we go out partying some time!

Everything about life in LA was good, and I had every reason to be completely happy. But I was far from it. I was going through some terrible problems at the time, because I couldn't cope with not having my kids living with me, not being able to see them. I was completely messed up, as low as I'd ever been. I'll never, ever be as low again as I was then. It was so traumatic. I was out in LA with Carolyne, whom I loved dearly and passionately, but I was still obsessed with Sharron, because if I had Sharron with me, then I'd have had my kids, too. I couldn't work out how I was going to deal with it.

The pain I was going through was indescribable. It was emotional pain, but it was very real, worse than any physical pain I'd ever experienced in the ring. It was gut-wrenching, my stomach was all tied up in knots, I couldn't focus or concentrate on anything. I lost count of the number of times I just broke down in uncontrollable floods of tears. I loved Carolyne so deeply, but my feelings were just ripping me apart, and I was causing her and myself so much hurt. The whole thing gnawed away at me, and I was so confused I didn't know what I was doing. I felt as though my heart was split in two, and I just couldn't deal with it. One moment I thought one thing, the next moment I thought another.

My mind turned to the darkest thoughts imaginable, and I started contemplating terrible things. I found myself wondering whether my life was worth all the excruciating pain I was suffering. Everything seemed worthless — the money, the fame, the success. I even thought about taking my own life. It seemed like an easy way out, an easy way to escape from the despair and frustration that I felt in every cell of my body. From the outside, my life may have seemed perfect; on the inside, I was weeping like a small child. What would I have done if I hadn't had Carolyne there to give me the love and support that I needed? I don't even want to think about it.

Carolyne and I were at loggerheads. We knew we couldn't go on like this. One day we were sitting down talking about it, and Carolyne just said, 'Nigel, you've tried everything — maybe you should just get hypnotised!'

We both laughed, but after a few seconds we looked at each other, and I thought, Hmm, maybe that's not such a crazy idea. And that's how it happened. I decided to try hypnosis to sort out my problems. It shows what a bad state I was in, because before that I'd never believed in hypnotism. Nobody's going to make me eat onion and tell me it's a fucking apple, do you know what I mean? And what if somebody puts me under and says, 'Nigel, put all your money into my account!' But I wanted it badly, and if anyone was going to hypnotise me, then I'd go to the best, so I called my agent and told him to get me an appointment with Paul McKenna.

We flew over from LA specially to see him in his offices in Kensington. Now, Paul McKenna had seen Nigel Benn whoop ass, so I don't know what he was expecting. He must have been a bit surprised, though, when he saw the state I was in when I walked into his office. I shook his hand, and said 'Paul, you gotta help me,' and then I just broke down in tears. I was a complete mess.

Paul must have been thinking, Christ, a few months ago I saw this man on telly knocking the shit out of some guy, and now he's a dribbling mess in my office! I was in such a state. But he put me under, and I can only remember a few details: Peter Pan's holding my hand, and I'm flying through the clouds. All I can hear are whale noises in the sea, and it's all so calm.

Afterwards, I tried to remember what he'd said to me, but I couldn't remember a single thing — I suppose I was just trying to put Sharron out of my mind.

When I woke up, Carolyne was there and she was in tears, complete floods of tears. I couldn't remember a thing, but she must have heard all the traumatic stuff I was coming out with. But you know, I wanted to be healed so badly that when I woke up I was a different man. Paul McKenna had helped me put the past behind me, and for that I want to thank him.

Afterwards, loads of people were saying that I'd gone to see Paul to help with my fighting. Complete bollocks! I don't need help like that from anyone when it comes to what goes on inside the ring. If a man has two arms, two legs and a heart like me, then I can deal with that. But when you break up with a woman, the mother of your kids — the pain is like nothing on earth. The knife's already in, and they can just turn it inch by inch. I don't care how hard you are, but when a woman starts twisting that knife, then the pain is unbearable. I'll go and fight Mike Tyson all day long, he could fuck me up, and I wouldn't care. You could get your ass beaten by Tyson — and you're still £5 million richer! So what? That kind of pain goes, you get compensated. But the pain a woman inflicts on you lingers for years.

McKenna healed that pain for me. I never had to go back, because he'd done what he had to do. And when I thanked him after the fight with McClellan, I was thanking him for putting my life back on course. I'll never get that low again.

Now, though, I was in the right frame of mind to start concentrating on the important business of my career. I was meant to fight Michael Nunn, but I was told, 'OK, Nigel, fight Michael Nunn. But it's an easy fight — you'll have to take £100,000 less.'

Excuse me? I'm the world champion, and they want me to take £100,000 less? I told them just what I was thinking — bollocks to that!

So they said to me, 'You don't fight Michael Nunn, but then you fight Gerald McClellan — a mini-Mike Tyson.'

'I don't give a fuck,' I told them. 'Bring him on! Bring him on, Don!' I don't know if I was supposed to be scared, but it just made me more determined than ever. It got my goat, and I just didn't want to fight anybody else. I wanted McClellan. Bring him on!

The hype about McClellan was amazing. He was being described as the most ferocious boxer ever to hit our shores, a freak of nature. Two things were at stake here — big money and my glory. I wanted both desperately, and I spent an intensive eight weeks of rigorous exercise in Tenerife to prepare for it.

He came over to Britain for the fight, and was giving it *large*. But by this time, I'd got into my training mode, and for this fight, it was more mental training that I needed. I was like, 'Right, mate. Don't think you're going to come over here and knock me out, not when I've got 20 million Brits on my side, supporting me all the way.' My mental and physical training had gone perfectly, absolutely perfectly. I kept thinking to myself, Have I missed anything, what have I missed? But I'd missed nothing. The running and the sparring had been bang on — not too much, because I'm not one of those guys who likes getting all bashed up sparring only to leave it all in the gym. Food, vitamins, sleep — bang on. I'd done everything.

I kept a low profile, and stayed totally focused on the job ahead of me. To my mind, McClellan was nothing more than an obstacle to me fulfilling my dreams. He was stopping my family from having the best things I could give them. He had to be removed.

When we met at the press conference, I just looked him straight in the eye; I'm ready for you, mate. I felt hard as nails, and no Yank was coming over to beat me on my home ground.

All the papers had me to lose. None of them had backed me to go past three rounds, except the *Star*. I didn't read them before the fight, but I read them all afterwards, so I knew who'd been predicting what. Not one of them said, 'Let's get behind our boy, let's give him the support he needs.'

But I had my support from Carolyne. When the white stretch limo arrived to pick me up for the fight, she didn't come outside to see me off. We'd kissed indoors and said how much we loved each other and I knew she was trying to hide her anxiety. I also knew she'd be there in the crowd at the fight. She didn't wish me luck. She knew I didn't need it.

As the limo neared the stadium, I felt like Spartacus going to the arena to fight to the death. The adrenalin was pumping hard, so hard I swear I could hear it. My blood was boiling and I was ready to swing some punches.

When I entered the ring that night, the atmosphere was electric. I looked across at McClellan and thought, 'Yeah, the arms don't look too bad, legs are skinny.' The noise from the crowd was like nothing I'd heard before, and all the hairs on the back of my neck stood on end. They booed McClellan, and they cheered me — 12,000 Brits right behind me. I thought to myself, How the fuck is he going to beat me here? OK, let's get this fight over with!

Once the bell goes, though, it's different. You might have 12,000 people behind you, but at the end of the day it's you and the other guy, alone in the ring — and neither of you want to give an inch. None of your supporters can help you, but sometimes you can feel them. You can feel their support, and it gives you a kind of strength that you don't get from anywhere else.

The round started, and he hit me. Yeah, that's not too bad, I thought. When he hit me again, though, I felt all the ligaments in the side of my neck rip, and I went out of the ring! Everyone was saying, 'We told you he'd do it. We told you he'd spark Benn in the first round.'

They wrote me off after that second punch, but I was like 'Excuse me! Excuse me! I'm getting up now!' And that was when I got back in the ring. I just thought, Fuck you, you're not beating me. I'm not lying down. I don't care how hard you hit — I've been hit with everything, pickaxes, baseball bats, so what? Let me see how you feel when I'm hitting you now.

But in that first round he carried on battering me around the place, trying to get me to end it.

When the bell finally sounded, my corner man Dennie Mancini took over the show. He grabbed me and said, 'Fucking hell, Nigel, you've really got him in trouble, mate!'

But I'm bashed to pieces! What's he talking about, I've got him in trouble? When I heard what Dennie said, though, it turned it all around for me.

'Really? Yeah, too right, Den, he is in trouble.' That was just what I needed to pick me up. If I'd had some guy in the corner saying, 'Look, Nige, you're taking a battering here,' then my morale's going to plummet. But thanks to Dennie, I went into the second round feeling like a champion, and now it's me bashing him around, me making him run. *Bang!* Come on, mate, I don't care what you throw at me.

By this time, my morale's high. I remember in the third round, though, he hit me with a body shot like I'd never felt before. If he'd done that again I'd have gone down, it hurt so much. But after I took that punch, I walked forward to show him 'Yeah, come on, then.' Really, I'm thinking, Please, don't hit me like that again! And he didn't, which gave me my energy back, and the ability to continue.

Round four, and his gumshield's hanging out of his mouth; he's exhausted. But I'm ready to go on. In round six, I sent his gumshield flying from his mouth, and it was clear I'd won the mental battle when, at the start of the seventh, McClellan stood up from his stool really slowly — he was tired. Even in round eight, when he put me down, I got straight back up and gave him a right uppercut and a left hook, and I said to him, 'When you come up for round fucking nine, there's going to be more of that.' We went back to our corners and whose heart's broken, his or mine?

When he went down in round ten, he'd taken two right-handers. I had a left hook ready but he was already on the floor — and he wasn't getting up. The whole place went wild and the noise was something else; the roof just came off. Gerald McClellan, pound for pound the hardest puncher in the world, the Yank who'd beaten Roy Jones as an amateur, was on the floor, and what made me proudest of all was this: it was a British man who'd done it, on his own turf.

I'd done it, and I felt good. Outside the ring, a TV interviewer came up to me, but I grabbed the microphone and spoke my mind.

'They just brought him over here to bash me up. Now I'm the man! Look at him now!'

By this time, though, I'm all bashed up myself, and everyone's coming up to me, patting me on the back. I couldn't take any more and I just blacked out and collapsed.

When I woke up I was in hospital in so much pain, with Carolyne beside me, crying her eyes out. Gerald McClellan was in the same hospital, so I went in to see him. If I thought I was in a bad state — I had a fractured nose and jaw, my kidneys were so damaged I was passing blood, and I had a shadow on the brain — then McClellan was twice as bad. He wasn't even awake. I went over to his bed, where I took his hand, kissed it, and simply said 'Sorry.'

When I got home, I had a couple of friends with me and they put me in the bath. I lay there for two hours, unable to move. I couldn't even get out by myself, so at about 4.00am, I had to call the guys and they lifted me out. When you're in that sort of state, shaking from pain as though you're going through cold turkey, you have to start wondering how much more you can take, how much more you can allow your body to be damaged to that extent. I'd always wanted my own little Rocky fight, and that had been it — blood and guts, excitement. But I'd never been hit like that before. I couldn't even eat, my mouth was so battered. My tongue was split right down both sides, and Carolyne had to try and feed me with just rice, but I couldn't even manage that. While my family were tucking into a roast dinner the next day, all I could manage was soup.

Up until that fight, my little daughter Sadé thought that my fights were staged, a bit like WWF wrestling. It was Carolyne who had had to tell her the truth about what her daddy did for a living.

'This is serious, Sadé,' she said to her.

'Can the same thing happen to Daddy that happened to Michael Watson?' Sadé asked innocently.

'Of course it can.'

After that conversation she came up to me and pleaded, 'Do you know what I really, really want, Daddy? More than anything?'

'What do you want, Darling?'

'I want you to stop fighting.'

I had a big lump in my throat when she said that to me, and that one simple request changed my life for ever. The fight game just wasn't the same any more.

18

WITH FRIENDS
LIKE THESE ...

After McClellan, I started thinking seriously about retiring. I'd always known the risks of getting into the ring with men like that, and so had he, but that fight really brought it home to me. It brought it home to my family, too. My kids started begging me to stop fighting, and so did Carolyne. I started to realise that every time I took a battering, so did they. I wanted out.

But that didn't mean I was going to take anything lying down, and although I was sorry for what had happened to McClellan, I thought his family were well out of order in the way they had behaved after the fight. In the pre-fight build-up, you should have heard the things they were saying about me — they wanted me dead. After the fight, though, it was a different matter.

'We wanted Benn dead, now we want his money.'

They wanted compensation from me for what happened to McClellan in the ring, but they were still bad-mouthing me.

If they want money, they can go to Don King — he's the man with the big bucks, he's the man who brought McClellan over to bash me up. I'm just trying to make an honest living to support my kids, and if they think I'm going to part with my money after hearing what they said about me — no way. I know for a fact that if I was in McClellan's shoes, my dad would handle it with some self-respect. Sure, he'd be upset, but he'd say, 'It happens. You're over 21. You knew what you were up against.' He wouldn't take it out on the other guy's family, and he wouldn't slag anybody off.

Although I was beginning to think about leaving the world of boxing behind me, I was still committed to a few more fights. The first was against the Italian Vincenzo Nardiello in July. The ironic thing was that in the match before us, Orlin Norris received the same treatment that McClellan had had from me.

When I got into the ring, though, it was business as usual. Nardiello was complaining about a slippery canvas, but I just kept quite about it — I wanted him to have a much closer view of that slippery canvas than I would! He gave me eight easy rounds before his corner threw in the white towel. To be honest, though, it wasn't my best performance. I remember saying at the time, 'Everybody deserves a bad day at the office, and that was mine!'

I stopped Danny Perez in the seventh on 2 September 1995. I didn't know it at the time, but that was to be my last victory. My belt was taken from me exactly six months later by Sugarboy Malinga on 2 March 1996. I'd trained so hard for that fight, but I don't know what happened to my performance. Perhaps I just left it all in the gym, or perhaps Malinga was just the kind of fighter who'd beat me all year round, the kind of player I couldn't deal with — I don't know. When I put him down in round five, I was just knackered. He wasn't in McClellan's class, and I thought I'd be in for an easy night of it. The hardest punch I'd ever felt was when Malinga hit me in the mouth. My teeth went through my gumshield and I actually felt them go

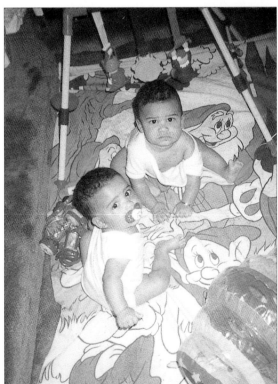

Top left: Soldier Benn in Minden, West Germany, 1982.
Top right: Brother Fusiliers: John Benn and me on exercises in Senalager, West Germany 1983.
Bottom: Two of the happiest days of my life were the day Carolyne became my wife, and the day our beautiful twins Conor and India were born.

Top: Super promoter Don King hugs 'my man Nigel'.
Bottom: At my luxury flat on the Thames with my beautiful daughter Renée, who was born on July 12, 1993. Dad is on the left!

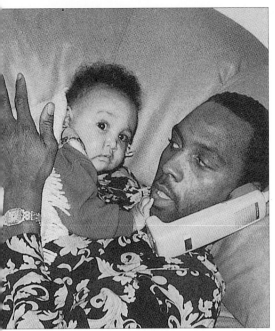

Top left: Relaxing with Renée.
Top right: Two mighty warriors – with the man himself, Mike Tyson in Las Vegas.
Bottom: With Jimmy Tibbs, the finest trainer I've ever had – although I do have a bone to pick with his son ...

Top left: High altitude training on Mount Tiede, Tenerife, where the film *Planet of the Apes* was shot. At a height of 8000 feet I would run up to 15 miles a day.
Top right: Weight training.
Bottom: Training in the ring – no matter what the fight, the work I put in was always 100%.

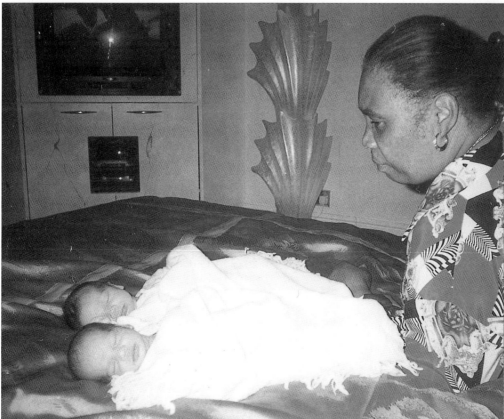

Top: My family mean everything to me now. This picture of me with Sadé, Renée and Dominic was taken in the back garden of our house.
Bottom: My mother with the twins.

Top Left: I spent three years in Miami. Here I am pictured in my open-top jeep.
Top Right: With Carolyne on our wedding day.
Bottom: When we were out in LA, I hit rock bottom. I will never get that low again. It was Carolyne who helped me out of it, and for that I owe her everything.

A trip to Disneyland. It was a happy day – you can see our smiles are as big as Mickey Mouse's!

Some of the best days of my life were spent at clubs like the Ministry of Sound. My new career is as a DJ – there's no bigger buzz than knowing that a big crowd is into your set.
Inset top: My good friend Wayne.
Inset bottom: At home with Conor.

through my tongue. I've still got the scar. Usually, you don't feel much until after the fight, but I felt that punch all right.

Looking back, I guess I just had nothing left. I was on my way down, but at the time you don't realise that. I just wanted to have a big fight, to show that I still had it, but when it came to the night I didn't even have the adrenalin rush I'd need to put in a good performance, and in the end he gave me a bashing. I lost on a decision, but still took home a purse of £800,000. The money was incidental, though. I was absolutely gutted, especially losing in front of all the Geordies, whom I love to death. I'd rather have lost to Eubank at Old Trafford than lost to Sugarboy Malinga on that night.

My last two fights were with Steve Collins on 6 July 1996 and then again on 9 November. For that last fight, I felt my pride was at stake, and I went there intending to win. Carolyne was in the audience with a friend, though, and had a premonition that I was going to lose that night, because as I got into the ring, I scanned the crowd and picked her out. I'd never, ever looked for her during a fight before, not throughout my entire career. When I saw her, I winked at her, and she just turned to her friend and said in a quiet voice that was almost drowned by the sound of the crowd, 'Nigel's going to lose tonight.' And that was my last fight.

I couldn't disagree with my corner when they threw in the towel as the bell rang for round seven. But I couldn't believe the reaction of the crowd. During the fight, they'd been cheering me on every time I got an opportunity. When I called it a day, they couldn't stop booing. But that didn't bother me — I knew I'd had enough, and I knew it was time to tell the crowd that they wouldn't be seeing me in the ring again. I threw my gloves towards the spectators, and grabbed the microphone.

'Can I have a few words, please?'

The crowd responded with booing.

Again, I asked, 'Can I have a few words?' Still the crowd booed.

It was then that Steve Collins stole the mike from me. 'Give him his due,' he shouted above the din. 'He's the greatest fighter in the history of British boxing!'

Now that got their attention. The crowd hushed as I took the microphone back.

'It's time to call it day,' I told them. 'The one thing I like doing is pleasing the British public. I can't take it any more. Thank you.'

And with that, I walked away from the ring. It was over, the end of a great career, and I felt good. I could look back on my life with pride, and enjoy the memory of what I had achieved. I had absolutely no regrets when I hung up my gloves that night — I'd made millions, I was famous, I was still young and I hadn't been bashed to a pulp. My head was still screwed on straight and I was madly in love.

I knew I wouldn't miss the gruelling training, the pain, the pre-fight nerves. But more than anything, I knew I wouldn't miss distressing the people I loved every time I stepped in the ring. And I knew that I wouldn't have to worry about money. Through my boxing, I'd earned something like £10 million — but at least £4 million of that had gone to the tax man. Still, there was money in the bank and I could afford to take it easy. I was looking forward to being able to spend some time with Carolyne and the kids. But if I thought I was in for a bit of peace and quiet, though, I couldn't be more wrong. Even after the Collins fight, after I'd retired, there were people ready to knock me.

For ages, Prince Nazeem Hamed had been mouthing off

about me. He came into my gym once in Tenerife, strutting around like he owned the place, and I had to tell him, 'Out, mate! Get out of my gym.' He was giving it large, and I just thought, 'Nah, mate, don't come in here, giving it all large. Show me some proper respect.'

He might have all those Mickey Mouse guys around him, licking his ass — 'Oh Nazeem, Nazeem!' — but he's not going to get that treatment from me. What a bunch of pricks! And then you see them carrying him into the ring, like he's some kind of king and they're his slaves. Have some respect for yourself!

And then, after the last Collins fight, he comes out in the papers slagging me off, saying, 'You can break my legs and rip my arms off, but I would still come out fighting.' What a load of shit — try it on with me, and *I* will break your legs and rip your arms off and, at the end of the day, the public caned him for what he was saying. Maybe if he'd done half of what I'd done they'd have taken their hat off to him, but they all know! I've fought everybody, but Hamed hasn't had nearly the same calibre of opponents. Everyone knows that there are fighters out there who will annihilate him, and he's just avoiding them. If you're meant to be the best in the world, Nazeem, then go and fight some of the top Americans. Prove yourself, like I did. Then you can run your mouth off. But in the boxing fraternity, we all know that he's fighting nobodies.

When I saw him at the Brit Awards, I gave him a piece of my mind: 'Let me tell you now, I'll punch you up in the air, you little shit.'

Does he reckon he wants to exchange punches with me? I'll screw him up in a little ball and throw him in the waste paper bin.

In fact, that evening at the Brit Awards was a funny one in other ways, too. I bumped into all sorts of people

— Robbie Williams being one of them. I'd met him before when we were on a flight back from Manchester together. Now, I'm not a great flyer at the best of times. In fact, I hate it. Give me 12 rounds with some big feller any time rather than a bumpy flight!

On that particular occasion with Robbie, there was some violent turbulence, and the plane was bouncing all over the place. So when the plane shook, I grabbed Robbie's hand! He must have thought, Hey, what's this big guy doing, grabbing my hand like that?

I just said, 'Sorry, mate,' but I'm thinking, What a fucking idiot! Oh, man, I can't believe I've just done that!

I manage to settle down, and then we go through another patch of turbulence, and I grab his hand again! I couldn't *believe* it.

So we're at the Brit Awards, and Carolyne's got me going up to all the stars asking for their autographs for the kids, and she plays this joke on me, saying that Robbie Williams knew I was around and wanted to have a chat. So we go to his dressing room and knock on the door — and it's only then that Carolyne tells me that he's not *really* been asking for me.

I'm like, 'Oh *no*, I don't believe it,' and then the door opens and some guy asks me what I want.

'Just tell Robbie that Nigel called round, will you?' I asked him.

'Yeah, sure mate,' said the guy at the door, obviously thinking I'm just some ordinary fan.

But later on, Robbie tracks me down.

'Nige, mate,' and we get on like a house on fire. I had to get him to go and tell the guy at the door who I was, though, because I was so embarrassed!

I also knew that Eubank was going to be there that evening, and I was ready to whack him if he came on all lairy with me. I meant it, too. My boxing days were finished, but if he came on with all that shit, I was ready to up him. So on the night, we found ourselves in the changing room, and my heart was beating hard because I thought he was going to come on all lairy.

But just the opposite happened. He came up to me, I shook his hand, and then he gives me a big hug! And that was it. I just thought, Wow, this is a different man. And we got on like a house on fire. I couldn't believe it — here was the man who'd said so many bad things about me, whom I'd caned in public, whom I'd been in the ring with in some of the most gruelling fights of my career, and we were chatting away backstage at the Brit Awards like old buddies. We even exchanged numbers, and he called me the next day. And a year ago we hated each other!

I don't really see him now, and we'll never get that close, but my opinion of him changed that night. Now I think, good luck to him, more power to the man. I can't knock a guy who'd defeated me. I've got to say, though, I still think he's a bit weird.

When I look back on my life, I realise that it's always been a bit like that. There are so many hangers-on that you can never tell who's your friend and who isn't. I'm not saying that Eubank and I are ever going to be like brothers, but things like that make you wonder whom you can trust. My whole boxing career has been a succession of people coming and going, and sometimes people really surprise you when they show their true colours.

Take Pete De Freitas, for example. When he started working with me we got on well, everything was cool. And when I was fighting, he lived the high life, flashing his gold cards everywhere, money rolling in largely because he was looking after Nigel Benn. He bought

Elton John's Bentley and all that. With a lot of people, they think they run the show but, at the end of the day, he was was a sort of gofer. He wanted to feel important. When I quit the ring after the last Steve Collins fight, he tried to persuade me to carry on in the fight game. By this time I'm all fucked up, I had all sorts of problems and stuff, but he still wanted me to go on. That's how we fell out.

Peter De Freitas is still helped by my name — I got a letter from him recently, all fucking grovelling and which he should be embarrassed to have sent me — it had my credentials on the letterhead! He used to have a big house, big car — now he's got shit.

He also thinks he's fucking hard but if he wants to try it on with me, he knows where I am, and he can come and find me. And I'll sort him out, because I was the one who helped to put him where he was.

Now he's looking after my two cousins who are in the fight game, and it's not something I'm happy about. If I had my way, they'd be with Frank Warren and Jimmy Tibbs, the best promoter and trainer in the business. I love Jimmy to death, even though we split before the end of my career.

Jimmy Tibbs's son, though, is a different kettle of fish. When I watched the video of the McClellan fight, I saw him appear to jump up and cheer my opponent when he put me down — I thought it was maybe because I didn't train with his dad any more. It doesn't bother me, though; I know I've achieved more in my life than he ever will. Things like that just make me more determined. My disagreement with Jimmy's son doesn't change how I feel about his dad though — he's the very best trainer I ever had, and my love and respect go out to him.

You can tell genuine people because they just say 'Hi,'

and then leave you alone. They're not on the make. Not that I mind chatting to members of the British public who come up to me in the street. They're the ones who put me where I am today, and if I can't spare a few minutes of my time to talk to them, then there must be something wrong with me.

I'm lucky to have come from such a loving, protective family. My brothers — I love them all to death, but they're all so different.

Dermot is the oldest. He used to work for me, and for my Dad, and he's a real grafter. He's a very happy-go-lucky guy, though, just going through life trying to enjoy himself without hurting anybody else. What he does need to do, though, is to learn to swim. He was round my house a while ago when we all ganged up on him and threw him in the pool. He starts swimming like the man from Atlantis —underwater! I had to jump in wearing all my clothes and rescue him! So that Christmas, all he got from his brothers was some armbands and a pair of flip-flops!

John I was in the army with, which I just loved. He's such fun to be around, really funny guy. But he works hard, too, a real law-abiding citizen. Danny's very quiet, but you know what they say about the quiet ones — silent, but deadly! He's just had a lovely little boy who he's called Orlando.

Mark's the real character of the family — a real Arthur Daley, making jokes about everyone and everything. I don't see him very often, which is a real shame. And Anthony, he's my kid brother and the real brain-box of the family. He's the most intelligent brother I've ever seen! I was so proud of him when I went to see him at his graduation, all decked out in one of those flat hats and everything. He's done so well for himself, I'll be asking him for sub soon! He spent a couple of years living at my house, a while back. The funniest thing about Anthony is that he's the spitting image of Lennox Lewis. People come up to him and ask him for his autograph, which sends him berserk — probably because he's not got Lennox's money!

But the people who've kept this tight-knit family unit together are my Mum and Dad. My Mum is the best in the world. She's spent so many years looking after people, that she doesn't like to be without kids all around her. She went through so much stuff when I was at school, I really put her through it, so I am so in debt to her. She has the most beautiful soul, my mother, the loveliest nature anyone could have.

And my Dad, he's the old power-house, he rules the roost. We argue like cats and dogs, sometimes, but at the end of the day he's always been the one that wants the best for me. All through my career he's been right behind me, weeding out the wrong 'uns, and making me get rid of them. He knows what he's talking about, my Dad — like with my trainers, the only one he ever really liked was Jimmy Tibbs, and there's no doubt he was right that Jimmy was my best ever trainer. He works hard, because he likes to keep his mind occupied. I'm lucky to have a Dad with such integrity, who speaks his mind and is always looking out for me.

These days, I do have to choose my friends more carefully. My wife Carolyne helps me to do that, and so does my agent, David Simones. David is a lovely, lovely guy whom I've known for a long time now. Never once has David tried to harm me, he has always been absolutely loyal, he always showed me utter respect and now eleven years down the road we're still together. He's a good man, and I love him to death. I'm also lucky enough to have good friends like Dave and Sandra Maddox, and my dear, dear friends Wayne and Karen.

Together, they've helped me forge my new life, one which is completely separate from my wild, wonderful, turbulent boxing career.

19

FAMILY MAN

My life has been a constant roller-coaster ride, full of ups and downs, not only in my career, but also in my personal life. I've reached heights of happiness and depths of depression. Things have happened to me in my life that make me want to laugh with joy, and other things have made me want to break down and cry — or worse.

At the centre of everything is Carolyne, the most wonderful, compassionate woman I have ever known. When I first met her, I knew that she was different in every way to the women I had known before. From the beginning, she was interested only in the real Nigel Benn, the man behind the image. So many people come up and want to be your friend because they want something from you. Carolyne never asked me for anything.

We have been through some terrible, traumatic times together, and she has always been there for me. Only Carolyne understands the pain I've been through — I'm not talking about the pain in the ring, but the unbearable emotional pain you feel in your soul when you find yourself caught in the whirlwind of feelings that can inflict themselves on the life of a man who loves his family more than life itself.

After I split from Sharron, my mind was in turmoil. The depth of my feelings for Carolyne was so strong, but so, too, was my love for my children, Dominic, Sadé and Renée, and half of me wanted my relationship with Sharron to work out, just for their sake. Man, it was ripping me apart. The pain was too much for me to bear. Throughout it all, Carolyne was there beside me. It was her that soaked up all the pain from me when I was going through my lowest point in LA. She took all the hurt from me.

There were times when I was so distraught I'd find myself going back to Sharron. When I think how much that must have hurt Carolyne, it makes me want to weep. But she took it in her stride, and she never did anything to make me think she was anything other than the most wonderful woman in the world.

On one occasion, out in LA, we went through one of those terrible traumatic patches. I told Carolyne that I wanted to try and make it work with Sharron, for the sake of the kids. Carolyne swallowed her pride and accepted it — she was upset, of course, but she acted in such an honourable way.

I had given a load of money — about £300,000 — to Carolyne to look after. After she'd flown back to England from LA, she wrote out a cheque for the money and gave it to my brother John. I was so messed up at the time that I never even thought about the money, but when John told me what she'd done, I was amazed. I've known so many people who would just have kept the cash — it made me realise what a special woman she was. Our split only lasted a week — I just didn't understand at the time how strong my love for her was.

And that wasn't the only time we'd broken up. On another occasion, I went out to Ibiza and Sharron was there, and I was in such a state I decided I wanted to try and work things out again. Carolyne decided to move out, but she packed all her clothes in black binliners because she didn't want to take anything from me — not even a few suitcases. I finally came to my senses, though, and tracked her down, and she moved back six weeks later.

Our relationship has been so tempestuous, like only the relationship between two people who love each other with all their heart can be. In the early years, it was especially volatile, but now the strength of our love has shown itself for what it is, and we live together with our family in such happiness.

A lot of people are trying to break me and Carolyne up, but it'll never happen. We'll never be parted, and I mean that — *never*. We're too much alike, and we understand each other perfectly. Even though I've made a lot of mistakes, my life would be meaningless without her. Since I've been with Carolyne, she's changed me dramatically. She's taught me about respect, and about loyalty — especially to women. She's instilled something profound and true within me, something I have to learn to make grow.

I sometimes think to myself, 'How would I ever deal with it if she left me?' I don't think I *could* deal with it. Now it's up to me. She's taken me as far as she can, and now I'm carrying on with my counselling again. I'm far from being mad, or anything like it, but sometimes I do things I regret — not physically, but mentally — and so often I end up hurting the woman I love, when she's never done me any harm. Maybe I'm still going through the transition from boyhood to manhood.

But despite the difficult periods, we've had some wonderful, happy times together, too. In the early days, we'd go to clubs and have a brilliant time. Now when I hear the music from those times, it brings it all back to me. They were some of the happiest times of my life. I'm always playing a track and saying, 'Hey, Carolyne, do you remember this one?' And she'll smile, and nod, and it'll remind us both of those days.

The most wonderful thing about Carolyne is how she looks after Dominic, Sadé and Renée, my kids by Sharron. My situation with Sharron is so difficult. When the kids go to see their mum, I hope she doesn't bad-mouth me. But kids grow up. Once, when I was slagging off Sharron, Sadé said, 'Don't say that, that's my mum you're talking about.' And from that day on, I've never said a word about Sharron to the kids. So as I say, one day the kids will grow up, and then they'll understand.

She's with a bloke called Clem now, and I've got no problem with him. My kids respect him and they talk about him in my house. If he spoke to me, I'd speak to him. No problem. But Sharron's another matter — I've even heard that she's been known to use my name to get into clubs and stuff. *My name*! So if you're reading my book, Sharron, don't use my name. Don't call yourself Mrs Benn! Clem's name is Clem St Clair, or something like that, not Clem St Benn!

In the middle of all this is Carolyne, my soulmate, my perfect woman. She was only a young woman when I met her — twenty years old. Suddenly she's having to take on my kids, court cases. I'm not going to get better than her, because she accepted my three kids as well as me. The most brilliant thing is how the kids love her, they really love her to death. When Carolyne said once that she was going away for a week, Sadé cried. She loves Carolyne badly — they all do. They've known each other since Dominic was about five. They were like babies when they first met, so now they really know her.

And she's never raised her hands to the kids, ever. She really shouts at them sometimes, and Sadé cries when she does, because she loves her so much, and she doesn't like upsetting her. Carolyne is like a mum to them, and gives them all her affection. I'm determined to give them the proper upbringing that they deserve.

I had to go through a terrible custody battle over the kids. I can't tell you how painful it was for me, having to get up in front of a judge and try to explain why my kids should live with me and not their mother. At the end of the court case, the judge gave me a really hard time — and Sharron, too. She was up in that dock for ages. And to make it worse, everyone knows about it. If a normal person has problems, they deal with it at home. If I have problems, everybody reads about it in the papers.

But Carolyne's helped me through all that. She is my backbone, and thanks to her I now have the most fantastic family life, living with five wonderful children. I also have another child, Harley, who was born after I had an affair with a dancer a few years back. He's a beautiful little boy, who I love very, very much.

Dominic is the eldest of my children who live with me. He's 12 now, and he's a big, strong boy — built like his dad! He's smart, too; I sit down with him, and try to teach him about life. I try to guide him in the right direction. I don't want to control his life, but I do want him and all the other kids to know that if they ever want my help, it's there for them. As and when they go out into the big wide world, I want them to have understood a bit from Dad. I've come up from the street — I got a degree in streetwise — and I want to pass a bit of that on to Dominic, so he knows he's not going out there blind. I don't know what the street's going to be like in another ten to fifteen years time, I don't even want to think about that, but I do want my kids to be prepared for it.

Deep down inside, Sadé is a very shy, sensitive girl. She's a really lovely person, and I can see that she hates hurting our feelings. Of all my kids, I think Sadé's the one who's feeling the whole relationship situation the most, but she's slowly growing out of it. She's definitely been the most affected by it, though. So with Sadé, you have to go easy on her — but you still have to be firm, because she's the kind of girl who could easily run wild if you let her go.

Renée is a beautiful, happy-go-lucky little girl, but she and Sadé fight all the time. They argue a lot, but if I see it happening, I have to come down hard. I don't know what happens in the other house, but I don't want to see two sisters who love each other fight so much. Any problems they've got between them, they leave at my doorstep. But little Renée, I love her to death, I really do.

Conor and India, Carolyne's and my twins, are just wonderful. The day they were born, 28 September 1996, I was the happiest man in the world. Ever since I'd been with Carolyne, we had so desperately wanted to have children together — at one stage we were having sex three times a day, just so that Carolyne would get pregnant. We took a trip to Hawaii so we could get away from everything, from our chaotic lifestyles, to relax and try for a baby. But it just wasn't working. She even had a course of IVF treatment which meant having to have injections every day, which added to the trauma we were experiencing. And as for me — on a few occasions, I started having what I can only describe as phantom pregnancies. I would become so sure that Carolyne was pregnant I'd find that I couldn't eat a thing. I was even having morning sickness — it was weird. Then, as soon as Carolyne started her period, I began eating again!

I can't even begin to describe the happiness I felt when Carolyne told me she was pregnant — and with twins. It was one of the most wonderful days of my life, and I literally had tears in my eyes. It was the one thing that Carolyne and I had been wishing for, the thing that would make our lives complete, and nothing could bring us off the cloud we were on.

The twins are so beautiful — Conor looks like me and

India looks like Carolyne. And it's so funny, watching the two together, it's just unbelievable. They're always together, playing, looking out for each other, looking after each other. When they were born they were so little — India was 4lb 3oz, and Conor was 5lb 7oz. Once, when they were really young, India was in bed, and she started trembling like a leaf. Conor started rocking his cot and looking over at India, who was shivering uncontrollably. I took India into my bed, but she was still shaking, so at about 5.00am I took her to the hospital. The doctor had to grab her leg to try to find a vein in her foot. India looked up at me, and her little eyes were saying, 'Daddy, daddy, it's hurting me!'

I just burst out crying, I didn't know what to do. I told the doctor, 'Hurry up, will you? Fucking hurry up!' I just lost it. When your kids are suffering like that, your mind goes. I know he was doing his job, but I was desperate — my daughter's looking me in the eye and saying, 'Daddy, he's hurting me, please stop him ...' It's enough to drive a man crazy!

I love our daily routine, in which I take the kids to school and pick them up again. I cook their dinner for them, everything. That's where I am at the moment, just caring for my beautiful wife and family.

Carolyne became my wife on 4 June 1997, and in that one simple act she gave meaning and direction to my life.

20

MINISTER OF SOUND

A lot of people soon get to the point where they just want to put on their slippers, stay at home and watch TV every night. That's not me. I don't want to be 60 and say I wish I had done this and that when I was 30. Just because you are married doesn't mean you have to start living like a married couple, where she does the needlework while you sit down with the crossword. And just because I'd finished boxing, it didn't mean I had no ambition left. I believe in living life to the full. When the grim reaper knocks on my door, I want to be able to say to him: 'Come on in, I've done everything I've ever wanted to do, come and take me. I have no regrets.'

The time when I was really living my life to the maximum was when I first got into the hardcore rave scene in the late Eighties. Man, they were good times. A while back I watched a TV programme on which all these hippies were talking about what it was like back in the Sixties. And the more I thought about it, the more I understood what they were saying. Those hippies had their time in the Sixties, while the Eighties and early Nineties — well, they were our time, my generation's party time, the time of the hardcore raves. Those hippies in the Sixties were all off their heads — well, it was just the same in the Eighties and Nineties.

Drugs have never been part of the scene for me, though. I don't want anything to do with them. I once tried some cocaine in America but that put me off for life. I sprinkled a bit on my finger and tasted it with my tongue but I wouldn't snort it. I don't agree with stuffing things up your nose. It would stop me from getting what I want in life. I'd rather have money in the bank.

Nothing upsets me more than when people say that I'm into drugs. Michael Watson made that mistake a couple of years ago. After Michael had been injured by Chris Eubank, I visited him in hospital. I just broke down and cried when I saw him, and it wasn't even me who'd inflicted the injuries. I took his mum shopping after the fight, and bought her loads of stuff. I just remember thinking that I hoped someone would do that to my mum if the same happened to me.

Just before Christmas 1993, Michael was robbed. Thieves ransacked his house, taking his TV and stereo and all his memorabilia and pictures. Everything. It was sick! I can't think of anything more low or disgusting. He was in a wheelchair and still suffering from brain damage. I would happily pay somebody a lot of money to tell me who it was. Michael was in tears when he told me about it. So I asked him round to my place for Christmas and bought him a replacement TV and stereo system.

So, one day we were talking on the phone, and he said to me, 'So, Nige, you off the gear?'

'What gear?'

'You know, the white gear ... the charlie.'

I couldn't believe what he was saying. 'Let me tell you something,' I said. 'I ain't never been on the gear to get off the fucking gear. Why you coming to me asking these questions? Where did you get this from?'

'I heard it from other people.'

'See you later, Michael,' I said, and put the phone down. I was really upset that Michael thought I might be doing that stuff. I've had plenty of offers, and there are plenty of boxers I know who've been on the Special K. Some of them have retired and some are still fighting — they know who they are without me naming them. I even confronted one guy with it when he was bad-mouthing me — and he was shoving charlie up his nose at the time! Not my scene, mate.

I haven't spoken to Michael since that day. I want him to know how much he upset me when he said that to me. Despite everything, I really love the man.

But drugs or no drugs, the scene was good in those days. We used to go to the Ministry of Sound, where there was a good crowd in the early days. Everybody knew everybody, and Master P was the DJ who was carrying it at the time. Sometimes we'd hang out at the Ministry until about 10.00am, then move on to The Bridge, The Park in Kensington and then on to the Café de Paris, which was *the* club. In those days, the DJs on the scene were guys like Justin Cantar, Micky Simms, and particularly Matt Jam. Those guys were carrying it on a US tip, the music was mellower, more like party music. These days it's all UK Underground, which is all attitude, much darker.

Nowadays, I don't really think of myself as a boxer any more — I think of myself as a DJ, and I strive to be as good a DJ as I can possibly be. Being a DJ is just as important in my life now as being a boxer ever was. This is my challenge now. I look up to the American guys, such as Louis Vega, Roger Sanchez, Dave Morales, CJ Mackintosh — men who are so tight, you can bet your bottom dollar that there's going to be no bump in the record when they're at the decks. When you listen to these guys mix, you just get lost and think, 'Please God, one day let me be able to be a quarter of what these guys are.'

In the same way that I was a world champion, these guys are world class, too. I'll never be number one like them, but as a DJ now, I'm just looking to give people a good time, and have fun myself. It's a big challenge for me, too, because the scene is full of people knocking me, saying I'm just getting off on my name to get the gigs. Well, let me tell you, I don't care who you are. If you've got the Queen mixing up at the Ministry of Sound, and she's screwing it up, you're off the decks, Ma'am! It doesn't matter who you are, you've got to be able to mix it, to get the crowd going, and if it ain't working, you ain't playing there again.

That's the level I'm at now — people can enjoy my music and come up to me and say, 'Yeah, wicked set, Nige!' I've got my decks set up in a room in my house, where I practise whenever I get the chance. I've got a set of Technics 1200 decks, and a Uri mixer — just like they have in the Ministry of Sound. Let me tell you, you've got to be tight to use a mixer like that — it's the complete guv'nor! There's no cross fader, so if you can't handle the mixer, there's no place to hide.

That's not what Frank Bruno thought, though, when we were both doing a set at this club in Birmingham. It was decided that there should be a Nigel Benn vs Frank Bruno DJ-ing competition. I thought it sounded like a laugh but, naturally, I wanted to be the champion! So I hit the deck and played a wicked two-hour set which really got the crowd rocking. I was pleased with it, and was like, 'Follow that, Frank!'

So it gets to Frank's turn, and he starts playing this monster set, really getting everyone moving. I was impressed, so I walked round to the decks only to see some other guy doing the mixing! Frank was even having a conversation with Carolyne. I don't think Frank asked to get paid for that gig.

Frank is funny like that — very, very funny. He had me

in fits of laughter once at a Buckingham Palace garden party by taking the mick out of everyone. The party was held to honour world champions, and I think Prince Edward represented the Queen. Frank had everyone around him rolling about with laughter. I always knew he was a joker, but when I saw him at the decks I couldn't believe it!

The music that I'm into now reminds me of those days gone by, those good times when everybody was happy. They were the happiest days of my life. And when I look back on it, I realise that one of the most important parts of my life back then was my relationship with Rolex Ray.

Ray and I were like brothers. I've never been as close to anyone as I was to him, and I never will be. We used to party hard together, and he always encouraged me in my boxing. In fact, it was Ray's encouragement and help that got me through a bad time after my first fight with Malinga. I was very down because although I had won on points, I was not very happy with the way it went. Ray took a more positive role and persuaded me to train with Jimmy Tibbs. I wasn't sure if Jimmy would want to train me, but Ray insisted on taking me round to his gym and I've never looked back since then. He also did the decent thing and insisted we speak first to my previous trainer and explain the position to him.

Some of the people I knew were hangers-on who tried to lead me astray because party time for them meant that I was footing the bill — even at the expense of my boxing. Now, Ray, I'm not saying he never led me astray, he just got me to party really hard. But he never let my partying interfere with the boxing; he always had respect for that. But the partying we did, Man! He'd hire out a whole penthouse suite at the Barbican just for us to have a good time. And he was heavily involved in the music with me — we used to go down to the Ministry of Sound at night, a whole group of us, just to practise our mixing. They were some hardcore days, some really happy days.

A lot of stuff has been written in the press about how Ray and I fell out, but he knows the truth, he knows how he ruined a good friendship. The whole episode is so hurtful to me. I was more upset about splitting with Ray than when Sharron and I separated. It was as though another brother had died. And now I'll never, ever speak to him again.

A couple of times a month I go out to Cyprus or Rhodes and DJ in the clubs out there, and it's in those places that I do most of my playing now. Like I've said, the UK Underground scene is much darker, full of guys with attitude, and I've got to put my family first. It's all down-in-the-dungeons music, and there's a lot of wannabe gangsters out there. I don't want to have to risk potentially violent situations, and if I'm in a club and somebody's disrespectful to my wife, then they're being disrespectful to me and I'm not going to take it. He'll inevitably come looking for me with a gun, I'll go looking for him with a gun — why would I want to be put in that position? Something can so easily go seriously wrong, but I love my wife and kids too much to let that happen.

So now I spend a lot of time at home, with my beautiful wife and five wonderful kids. I love being at home with them, and we have a lot of fun together. When Dominic and I battle it out for football supremacy on Playstation, I'm just as competitive as I was with Eubank! And Dominic, even though he is disabled and only has the use of one hand, has the heart of a sportsman — and can even whoop my ass from time to time!

I love my kids — they are the focus of my life now. But I'm strict with them just as my dad was strict with me. Since they've been living with me, their marks at school have gone through the roof, and that's because I make them work. I wouldn't want Conor to be a boxer — I went through that so he wouldn't have to. But they are going to have to graft just like I did, because I want them, like me, to be satisfied with their lives and what they've achieved.

When I look back over my life, I feel proud at what I've done, and now I feel so lucky to be surrounded by the people I love. I don't miss the fight game, because my life is as full now as it has ever been, but not a day goes by that I don't think about it, relive my victories, consider the highs and lows of my turbulent career. I've come a long way since I was a kid on the streets of Ilford. Nigel Gregory Benn, the Dark Destroyer, two-time champion of the world, 42-5-1. That's a good record, a career to be proud of. And if anyone wants to disagree — well, then, they'll have me to argue with.

BOXING RECORD

Nigel Gregory Benn

Super-Middleweight
Born 22 January 1964 in Ilford
West Ham ABC
Amateur: 1986 London and ABA middleweight champion

Professional

1987

Jun 28	Graeme Ahmed	W rsf 2 Croydon
Mar 4	Kevin Roper	W rsf 1 Basildon
Apr 22	Bob Nieuwenhuizen	W rsf 1 Albert Hall
May 9	Winston Burnett	W rsf 4 Battersea
Jun 17	Reginald Marks	W rsf 1 Albert Hall
Jul 1	Leon Morris	W ko 1 Albert Hall
Aug 9	Eddie Smith	W ko 1 Windsor
Sep 16	Winston Burnett	W rsf 3 Albert Hall
Oct 18	Russell Barke	W rsf 1 Windsor
Nov 3	Ronnie Yeo	W rsf 1 Bethnal Green
Nov 24	Ian Chantler	W ko 1 Wisbech
Dec 2	Reggie Miller	W ko 7 Albert Hall

1988

Jan 27	Fermin Cirinos	W ko 2 Bethnal Green
Feb 7	Byron Prince	W rsf 2 Stafford
Feb 24	Greg Taylor	W rsf 2 Abervanon
Mar 14	Darren Hobson	W ko 1 Norwich
Apr 20	Abdul Umaru Sanda	W rsf 2 Muswell Hill
May 28	Tim Williams	W rsf 2 Albert Hall
Oct 26	Anthony Logan	W ko 2 Albert Hall
Dec 10	David Noel	W rsf 1 Crystal Palace

1989

Feb 8	Mike Chilambe	W ko 1 Albert Hall
Mar 28	Mbayo Wa Mbayo	W ko 2 Glasgow
May 21	Michael Watson	L ko 6 Finsbury Park
Oct 20	Jorge Amparo	W pts 10 Atlantic City
Dec 1	Jose Quinones	W rsf 1 Las Vegas

1990

Jan 14	Sanderline Williams	W pts 10 Atlantic City
Apr 29	Doug De Witt	W rsf 8 Atlantic City
Aug 18	Iran Barkley	W rsf 1 Las Vegas
Nov 18	Chris Eubank	L rsf 9 Birmingham

1991

Apr 3	Robbie Sims	W rsf 7 Bethnal Green
Jul 3	Kid Milo	W rsf 4 Brentwood
Oct 26	Lenzie Morgan	W pts 10 Brentwood
Dec 7	Hector Lescano	W ko 3 Manchester

1992

Feb 19	Dan Sherry	W rsf 3 Muswell Hill
May 23	Sugarboy Malinga	W pts 10 Birmingham
Oct 3	Mauro Galvano	W rsf 3 Marino
Dec 12	Nicky Piper	W rsf 11 Muswell Hill

1993

Mar 6	Mauro Galvano	W pts 12 Glasgow
Jun 26	Lou Gent	W rsf 4 Olympia
Oct 9	Chris Eubank	DREW 12 Manchester

1994

Feb 26	Henry Wharton	W pts 12 Earls Court
Sep 10	Juan Giminez	W pts 12 Birmingham

1995

Feb 25	Gerald McClellan	W ko 10 London Arena
Jul 22	Vincenzo Nardiello	W rsf 8 London Arena
Sep 2	Danny Perez	W rsf 7 Wembly

1996

Mar 2	Sugarboy Malinga	L pts 12 Newcastle
July 6	Steve Collins	L rsf 4 Manchester
Nov 9	Steve Collins	L rsf 6 Manchester